BUSINESS BUILDERS IN BROADCASTING

On June 1, 1980, Ted Turner's CNN cable station began broadcasting news programs 24 hours a day.

BUSINESS BUILDERS IN BROADCASTING
BUSINESS BUILDERS IN COMPUTERS
BUSINESS BUILDERS IN COSMETICS
BUSINESS BUILDERS IN FASHION
BUSINESS BUILDERS IN FAST FOOD
BUSINESS BUILDERS IN OIL
BUSINESS BUILDERS IN REAL ESTATE
BUSINESS BUILDERS IN SWEETS AND TREATS
BUSINESS BUILDERS IN TOYS AND GAMES

BUSINESS BUILDERS
IN BROADCASTING

Nathan Aaseng

The Oliver Press, Inc.
Minneapolis

The Oliver Press, Inc.
Charlotte Square
5707 West 36th Street
Minneapolis, MN 55416-2510

Library of Congress Cataloging-in-Publication Data
Aaseng, Nathan.
Business builders in broadcasting / Nathan Aaseng
v. cm. — (Business builders ; 8)
Includes bibliographical references and index.
Contents: David Sarnoff: the NBC founder and his vision — William Paley: the master sales-
man at CBS — Gerald Levin: HBO: the first cable channel — Ted Turner: creator of CNN —
Rupert Murdoch: builder of the News Corporation — Catherine Hughes: Radio One: voice of
the black community — Judy McGrath: MTV and teenage culture.

1-881508-83-8 (library binding)
1. Broadcasting—United States—Biography—Juvenile literature. 2. Telecommunication—
United States—Biography—Juvenile literature. [1. Broadcasting. 2. Telecommunication. 3.
Businesspeople.] I. Title. II. Series.

HE8689.8.A56 2004
384.54'092'2—dc22
                              2003064982

ISBN 1-881508-83-8
Printed in the United States of America

11 10 09 08 07 06 05   8 7 6 5 4 3 2 1

CONTENTS

INTRODUCTION

THE BEGINNINGS OF BROADCASTING

In 1910, Dr. Hawley Crippen of Great Britain was literally getting away with murder. One step ahead of the law after killing his wife, he had managed to board the ocean liner *Montrose* before the authorities could catch up with him. Accompanied by his lover, Ethel le Neve, Crippen was now bound for North America, where he could disappear from sight and justice would never be served.

Crippen believed himself to be in the clear, but he failed to take into account advances in radio science. The *Montrose* was one of the first ships equipped for wireless communications. The ship's captain, Henry Kendall, grew suspicious of Crippen and le Neve (who was disguised as a boy). Kendall checked the descriptions of wanted criminals and transmitted a

The new wireless communication helped Scotland Yard capture murder suspect Dr. Hawley Crippen, who fled Europe aboard the Montrose. Reporters also used this new technology to cover the transatlantic chase, so photographers were on hand to record this image of the police leading Crippen off the ship.

wireless message to Scotland Yard. The inspector on the case, Walter C. Dew, boarded a faster ship and pursued the suspect. Dew and the captain were able to stay in contact during the chase and arrange a rendezvous point. Dew caught up with the *Montrose* and arrested Crippen. It was one of the first practical examples of what wireless communication—the sending and receiving of electronic signals through the atmosphere—could do for society.

LONG-DISTANCE COMMUNICATION

The first method of instant long-distance communication was probably drums, commonly used in Africa for centuries. Systems that used visual signals such as flags or smoke were also developed. Relay communication, such as the Pony Express service in the United States, was another method. But for thousands of years, the transmission of messages was limited to how far humans could hear sound, how far they could see signals, or how fast they could travel. When scientists began to unravel the mysteries of electricity in the late eighteenth and early nineteen centuries, however, their discoveries paved the way for modern communications.

Italian physicist Alessandro Volta (1745-1827) made the first electric battery in 1800. This device produced a steady flow of electric current, allowing scientists to experiment with electricity. Michael Faraday (1791-1867) in Great Britain and Joseph Henry (1797-1878) in the United States both contributed important discoveries about how electricity works.

radio: a device used to transmit and receive electronic signals (radio waves)

electricity: power generated by the interactions of positively and negatively charged particles (protons and electrons) in atoms

battery: connected cells that produce an electric current by converting chemical energy into electrical energy

8

In 1820, Danish physicist Hans Christian Oersted (1777-1851) discovered the magnetic effect of an electric current. Samuel Morse, along with several European inventors, built upon this principle to invent the telegraph in the early 1830s. Using a code based on long and short bursts of current, called dashes and dots, they created a method of sending messages through electrical wires. This new method of communication proved so popular that within 10 years of Morse's successful demonstration of his telegraph, more than 50 telegraph companies were in operation. In 1876, several inventors, the most prominent of whom was Alexander Graham Bell (1847-1922), improved upon this long-distance communication system by transmitting voices electronically over wires through a telephone.

Samuel Finley Breese Morse (1791-1872) posed with his electric telegraph.

Sir Oliver Lodge (1851-1940) was a physics professor as well as a pioneer in the new field of radio communications.

electromagnetic wave: a wave of electrical and magnetic energy that travels through space. Light waves, radio waves, and X rays are all electromagnetic waves.

wavelength: the distance between the peak of one wave and the peak of the next corresponding wave

WIRELESS COMMUNICATION

While these were tremendous improvements in communication, the technology was limited by its dependence on wires to link the sender and the receiver. In the meantime, people were discovering that it was possible to send electronic signals across air. In 1873, Scottish physicist James Clerk Maxwell (1831-1879) proved mathematically that it was theoretically possible to send such impulses using electromagnetic waves. Fourteen years later, Heinrich Hertz (1857-1894) of Germany demonstrated that these invisible waves, called radio waves, actually did exist, that they could travel at the speed of light, and that they could be bent in various directions. Continuing the international effort to harness radio waves, Great Britain's Sir Oliver Lodge, in 1890, developed a transmitter of radio waves and a crude receiver. The receiver could be matched or tuned to the same wavelength as the transmitted wave, capturing the transmission over a very short distance. Five years later, Alexander Stepanovich Popov (1859-1905) added an antenna to Lodge's receiver.

But no one had come up with any practical way of using this new knowledge about wireless communication until an Italian named Guglielmo Marconi (1874-1937) began experimenting in earnest in the 1890s. Financed by his father's fortune, Marconi gradually improved wireless transmission so that it was effective over greater distances. By 1895, he could receive radio transmissions more than one

mile away from the transmitter. Having failed to interest the Italian government in his project, he moved to England and founded the Wireless Telegraph and Signal Company in 1897.

By 1899, Marconi was able to send wireless messages across the English channel. Two years later, the letter *s* in Morse code (three dashes) was sent 2,140 miles across the Atlantic Ocean from Cornwall, England, to the coast of Newfoundland, Canada. While Marconi was perfecting his system,

In December 1901, Guglielmo Marconi (center, with two assistants) received a radio signal in Newfoundland, Canada, that had been sent across the Atlantic Ocean.

other inventors worked on ways to transmit more than dots and dashes. Karl F. Braun (1850-1918) came up with the cathode-ray tube, a specialized vacuum tube that could accelerate electrons in the form of a narrow beam. One of Marconi's colleagues, Sir John Ambrose Fleming (1849-1945), improved the detector, the device that received messages. His "Fleming valve" could carry the human voice or even music. This was followed in 1907 by American Lee de Forest's (1873-1961) audion. A vacuum tube with three electrodes instead of the usual two, it could amplify, or strengthen, radio waves as they were received. These inventions made possible long-range reception of radio signals.

The tiny Fleming valve, only a few inches long, revolutionized wireless technology.

The basis was now laid for wireless communication on a large scale. But as with most new technology, there was some uncertainty about how to use it. One of the first practical applications was safety on the ocean. The sinking of the luxury ship *Titanic* on April 15, 1912, created a great demand for increased use of wireless communications. Noting that hundreds of the 1,503 who died in the disaster could have been saved had the *Titanic* been able to contact a nearby vessel, the United States and Western European countries began requiring that ships crossing the Atlantic be equipped with wireless sets and have an operator on duty at all times.

WIRELESS GOES PUBLIC

The idea of transmitting information via wireless to the general public evolved slowly as radio technology improved. One early radio inventor, Canadian

Reginald Fessenden (1866-1932), aired Christmas greetings and music to ships on the Atlantic Ocean over a transmitter from Brant Rock, Massachusetts, on December 24, 1906.

Over the next several years, various inventors and amateur radio operators in both the United States and Europe tried their hand at communicating with others through radio waves. The first regularly scheduled and aired program was probably produced in 1909 by Charles Harold of the College of Engineering and Wireless in San Jose, California. As a practical application of the school's curriculum, Harold broadcast news reports and selections of music. So many others followed suit that the U.S. Congress recognized the need for some sort of organization and regulation of the airwaves. It passed the Radio Act of 1912, which assigned three- and four-letter codes to radio stations and limited the range of radio waves broadcasters could use. The act, however, failed to provide firm regulation of the allocation of broadcast frequency or of the hours and power of transmissions, and there was great chaos for years.

During World War I, the U.S. government shut down all the nation's radio stations so that they would not interfere with military communications. Following the war, there was strong sentiment in favor of the government assuming control of the operation of radio stations, as most governments had done in Europe. Broadcasting in the United States, however, was to go in a different direction, that of

Radio pioneer Reginald Fessenden (1866-1932)

frequency: the number of times a specific phenomenon—such as an electromagnetic wave pulse—repeats itself in one second

13

private ownership, although initially under the watchful eye and control of the government.

COMMERCIAL BROADCASTING

The beginnings of commercial broadcasting can be traced back to Frank Conrad, an engineer for the giant electrical corporation Westinghouse. In 1916 Conrad obtained an amateur license from the government for an experimental station in Pittsburgh. On October 17, 1916, he put a microphone in front of a phonograph and broadcast the music it played. Before long, amateur radio operators who happened

Frank Conrad (1874-1941) holds one of the radio tubes that made his early broadcasts possible.

to be listening began sending in requests for songs. Eventually, so many requests came in that Conrad stopped trying to fill them individually and instead began broadcasting a two-hour program of recorded music each Wednesday and Sunday.

Conrad provided all this as a public service. But in the summer of 1920, a local electronics company took advantage of the shows' popularity and advertised its radios as a way to obtain them. Those ads attracted the attention of Westinghouse officials, who were looking for ways to market the radios they were making. The company decided to start a radio station, provide programming, and advertise these programs to the public, who would then want to buy Westinghouse radios. In November 1920, its new station, KDKA, went on the air, broadcasting the presidential election returns to its listeners.

Over the next several years, radio broadcasting became a national phenomenon. In 1922 there were 100,000 radios produced in the country. A year later, 500,000 were made. By 1924, more than three million radios had been sold in the United States. The number of radio stations took a similar jump. In 1922 there were only 30 throughout the country; a year later there were more than 550.

license: to grant another the right to produce and sell an invention for a fee

station: a broadcast organization equipped to transmit radio or television signals; also refers to the frequency assigned to a broadcaster

LOOKING FOR IDENTITY

As the radio industry struggled to find its identity, it fell into chaos. There were so many radio stations in some cities that they were forced to share wavelengths, which meant that each station might be on the air for only a couple of hours a day. As customers became more selective about what they would listen to, programming competition became fierce. Those musical artists most in demand began asking for payment in exchange for performing over the airwaves. In the mad rush to make use of this wonderful new tool of mass communication, no one had yet solved the problem of how to generate the money needed for both equipment and performers. As a result, in 1923 more than 150 new stations went off the air.

Bell AT&T, the huge telephone company, tried to solve the money problem with a system of toll broadcasting—charging customers for the time they listened to the radio. The plan, however, was so unworkable that Bell abandoned it and sold all of its stations. It was left to the business builders featured in this book to solve the problem of how to pay for this new form of mass communication, the radio, and for the next mass communication device that followed, the television.

From the earliest days, social commentators recognized that broadcasting held almost limitless potential to be either a positive or negative force in society. Upon seeing television for the first time in 1939 at the New York World's Fair, author E. B. White wrote, "I believe television is going to be the test of the modern world, and that in this new opportunity to see beyond the range of our vision, we shall discover a new and unbearable disturbance of the modern peace, or a saving radiance in the sky. We shall stand or fall by television—of that I am quite sure."

television: a device that receives an electronic signal and converts that signal into an image

"Television? The word is half Greek and half Latin. No good will come of it." —*Manchester Guardian*

The word "television" comes from the Greek word for "far" and the Latin for "seeing" and was used as early as 1900.

Television and radio have indeed become dominating forces in the world; they shape billions of lives in every corner of the earth. Some view them as an "unbearable disturbance of the peace" or, as Federal Communications Commission chair Newton Minow called television in 1961, "a vast wasteland." Others view broadcasting as a "saving radiance in the sky" that has helped bring democracy to the world. In either case, the entrepreneurs introduced in this book are some of the people primarily responsible for making broadcasting what it is today.

A family in the 1950s enjoying the popular pastime of watching television

The FCC: Broadcasting's Watchdog

The development of radio technology posed a new problem for governments. How do you establish ownership or regulation of an invisible wave that travels through the air? If there were no controls or regulations, the limited number of radio wave bands would quickly be so crowded that everything that came across the radio would be a jumbled mess.

Congress took its first tentative steps toward radio regulation with the Radio Act of 1912. Under this provision, the Commerce Department assigned three- and four-letter station codes, but the law provided little oversight of the rapidly expanding industry. There was no authority designated to allocate frequency or regulate the hours or power of transmission, causing stations to interfere with one another's broadcasts.

In response to this void, Congress passed the Radio Act of 1927. The act contained several key ideas that remain important in the twenty-first century: the public owned the radio spectrum but individuals could be licensed to use that spectrum for the public interest, the broadcaster would be responsible for the content transmitted, and radio was protected by the First Amendment (the right to free speech). The act created a five-member Federal Radio Commission (FRC), an independent government agency answering to Congress, that would oversee the broadcasting industry. Each member of the FRC was responsible for administering a different region of the nation.

On June 19, 1934, Congress passed the Communications Act, replacing the FRC with the Federal Communications Commission (FCC), whose job was to enforce regulations that guarantee equal access and open competition in broadcasting. The FCC regulates broadcast licenses, specifying the location, channel, and operational power of the station. Originally, the FCC consisted of seven members; in 1983 the commission was cut to five. All members are appointed by the president with the approval of the Senate, and in an effort to avoid political abuse of the powerful tool of communications, no more than three members can be from the same political party.

The Communications Act has been altered several times, giving the FCC regulation over the new technologies that followed radio, including television, cable television, satellite and microwave communications, and cellular telephones. As in the past, the FCC has virtually no say in determining what can be broadcast. The three exceptions to that policy are restrictions on the number of commercials allowed during children's shows, rules against obscene and profane language, and the Equal Time Rule, requiring broadcasters to give equal opportunity to candidates for political office.

A group of people listen to an early radio broadcast in a hotel lobby.

1

DAVID SARNOFF

THE NBC FOUNDER
AND HIS VISION

Ironically, the man who created network broadcasting in the United States had little interest in the entertainment and news that he ushered onto the center stage of society. David Sarnoff never even bothered to meet the celebrities whose careers he launched. What fascinated him was the technology involved in carrying voices and images over the airwaves. Throughout his life, Sarnoff was first and foremost a manufacturer of radio equipment, with which he constantly tinkered in an effort to improve its quality.

Sarnoff recognized early in his career, however, that the best technology in the world would not entice customers to buy his radios unless there was something on the radio that they wanted to hear.

network: a chain of radio or television broadcasting stations linked together, or the company that produces the programs for these stations

The life of David Sarnoff (1891-1971) was a real rags-to-riches story. He began his career delivering telegraph messages and ended up head of NBC. Along the way, he greatly influenced both the technology and the business of broadcasting.

He developed the National Broadcasting Company (NBC) to provide programs that would give people a reason to buy his radios. He saw the comedy, music, sports, and news programs he created and distributed across the nation as basically sales tools.

A YOUNG BOY'S BURDEN

David Sarnoff, the oldest son of Abraham and Leah Sarnoff, was born on February 27, 1891, in Uzlian, Russia, near the city of Minsk. Abraham struggled to make a living as a house painter and saw little chance for any improvement in the family's economic condition. In 1896, he made a bold decision and sailed to the United States. He hoped that if he worked hard enough he could quickly earn the money to allow the rest of the family to join him. Meanwhile, David was sent to live with his great-uncle, who was a rabbi, to study the Jewish religion. His rigorous training allowed him no time for friends or games.

Abraham Sarnoff found little opportunity in America. Working long hours at low-paying jobs and living in squalor, it took him more than four years to acquire the money to send for his family. In 1900, nine-year-old David arrived in the United States only to find his father's health and will had been broken by the long struggle to earn their passage. David realized that much of the burden of caring for the family rested with him. "It was like being tossed into a whirlpool—a slum whirlpool—and left to sink or swim," he later recalled. Although he knew no English at first, David got a job selling newspapers. Eventually he saved up enough money

"It took Abraham Sarnoff four years to gather the $144 necessary to bring his family to America (a place in steerage cost $36). During that time, he endured a tenement room with three other men and destroyed what remained of his health in the untold hardships of menial jobs."
—Tom Lewis, author of *Empire of the Air*

to buy a newsstand of his own. At the same time, he attended elementary school at the Educational Alliance, a community organization run mostly by volunteers, where English became his favorite subject.

By the time David reached the age of 15, his father's health had declined to the point where David was the sole support of the family. The part-time newspaper business was no longer enough; David had to drop out of school to work full time. Intending to apply for a job at the office of the New York *Herald* newspaper, he mistakenly entered the office of the Commercial Cable Company, which was located in the same building as the *Herald* and was under the same management. (At this time, cable was another word for telegraph.) The cable company happened to be looking for a messenger boy. David worked for nine months at the job, pedaling a bicycle to deliver messages, before quitting in protest when his employer refused to give him time off to observe Jewish holidays.

TELEGRAPH OPERATOR

During those nine months, however, David Sarnoff became intrigued with the workings of cable communications; he even bought himself a telegraph key and learned Morse code. This fascination led him to a new job as an office boy at American Marconi Wireless Telegraph Company, the tiny U.S. branch of the company run by the great inventor Guglielmo Marconi. In between sweeping floors and running errands, Sarnoff learned everything he could about the technology and business of sending telegraph

telegraph key: the hand tool used by a telegraph operator to tap out a Morse code message

messages. His dedication was noticed by Marconi, who used Sarnoff as his personal messenger boy. In 1907, Marconi promoted Sarnoff to the position of junior wireless operator.

Sarnoff continued to rise in the company, first as a telegraph operator on ships and at land-based stations and later as a manager of a Marconi wireless station high atop the famous Wanamaker department store in New York City. The Wanamaker position gave rise to a legend that brought Sarnoff national hero status. According to the story, on April 14, 1912, he was on duty at his radio when the first report came in of the foundering of the spectacular luxury liner *Titanic*. Sarnoff supposedly remained at his post for 72 hours, staying in contact with the rescue ships until he was able to relay to relatives the name of the last *Titanic* survivor. But the first report was heard at a station in Newfoundland, Canada, and the Wanamaker building was most likely closed the Sunday evening the *Titanic* sank. So Sarnoff had created his own legend. It was a legend based in fact, however, because during the days following the disaster the Marconi stations were all busy relaying news and Sarnoff was part of that effort.

The tremendous loss of life in the *Titanic* tragedy, due partially to a lack of reliable communications, clearly demonstrated to Sarnoff the importance of wireless radio. He had been taking correspondence courses in engineering, but the more he thought of potential uses for the wireless device, the more excited he grew over the possibilities of guiding the

"'The *Titanic* disaster brought radio to the front,' Sarnoff was fond of saying in later years, 'and also me.' He was right. The *Titanic*'s wireless distress call was heard 58 miles away by the Marconi operator on the *Carpathia*, which enabled those in lifeboats to be rescued three and a half hours later. . . . But inadequate wireless installations on two other ships in the vicinity (which were in fact closer than the *Carpathia*) meant that the *Titanic*'s distress signal . . . went unheeded [by the closer ships]."
—Tom Lewis, author of *Empire of the Air*

Above: David Sarnoff working at a Marconi wireless station sometime in 1908

Left: A huge crowd outside the shipping company that owned the Titanic waits for the latest news. Others gathered at telegraph offices. "I've witnessed the most harrowing scenes of frantic people coming . . . to beg us to find out if there might not be some hope for their relations," wrote Guglielmo Marconi to his wife in Italy. He was in New York when the Titanic sank and, in fact, had bought a ticket to return home on the ship.

growth of a company. By 1914, Sarnoff gave up his engineering pursuits to concentrate solely on management within the Marconi Company.

RADIO VISION

Sarnoff was especially interested in a new type of radio receiver being developed by Edwin Armstrong, a young engineer whom he had met the previous year. He began to probe the possibility of using the improved technology to send music into remote locations. Prior to Sarnoff's involvement, wireless technology was primarily the domain of professionals and amateur enthusiasts. But Sarnoff believed that radio could be engineered to benefit the average citizen with no radio expertise at all. In 1914, he experimented with this notion by transmitting music from a phonograph into Wanamaker's Philadelphia department store for the benefit of customers. It was just a short step from there to imagining the possibilities of bringing music into homes across the nation.

In the fall of 1916, Sarnoff wrote a memo in which he described his vision of the radio as a "household utility." As he saw it, the wireless receiver could "be designed in the form of a simple 'Radio Music Box,' and arranged for several different wave lengths, which should be changeable with the throwing of a single switch or pressing of a single button." Under such a system, he believed it should be possible for hundreds of thousands of homes to receive a signal from a single transmitter. In addition to music, Sarnoff saw that news could be distributed almost instantly throughout a region, and that live descriptions of sporting events could provide listeners with the next-best experience to actually being at the event.

From time to time, others had made isolated attempts to turn radio into a commercial venture, but without success. Radio technology simply was not good enough; reception was often garbled and receivers had difficulty matching the frequencies of the transmitters. Under such conditions, most industry experts regarded attempts to create a mass radio market as commercial folly. But Sarnoff believed the technology would soon be developed, and he wanted to make certain that when radio became a vital part of society, as he predicted it would, his company would be positioned to ride the huge crest of sales that would result.

RCA

In the meantime, the Marconi Company, under the expert guidance of administrators such as Sarnoff, enjoyed a series of favorable breaks. Fresh from the experience of fighting World War I in Europe, the U.S. military had seen the vital need for fast, accurate, and widespread communication in the field. It lobbied for the creation of a powerful telecommunications company to create a broadcasting system that would give the U.S. a communications advantage over its enemies. In October 1919, electronics giant General Electric, which had recently absorbed Marconi's United States operations, formed a new business, Radio Corporation of America (RCA), to

telecommunications: the electronic systems used to transmit messages by cable, radio, telegraph, telephone, and television

create technology in response to this need. In cooperation with two other huge companies—electronics pioneer Westinghouse and telephone powerhouse American Telephone and Telegraph (AT&T)—RCA began setting up facilities capable of transmitting wireless broadcasting over wide areas.

David Sarnoff recognized that, regardless of the government's interest in the venture, RCA's survival ultimately depended on its ability to sell radios. The number of amateur radio buffs in the nation was limited, so he focused his efforts on attracting the average American consumer. Such customers would buy radios only if there were something of great interest being transmitted, if the technology required no specialized knowledge of electronics, and if the quality of the reception was high. The latter two were engineering problems that Sarnoff's company was able to solve, with a huge assist from his friend Edwin Armstrong. In 1920, Sarnoff bought Armstrong's patents for a device that made precise tuning of receivers a simple matter and for a radio vacuum tube that greatly enhanced reception. With Armstrong's improvements, refined by RCA engineers, RCA was able to create a virtual monopoly on mass-market radio receivers.

The problem of programming, however, was trickier. RCA was in the business of electronics, not entertainment, news, or sports. But very few others were offering programs of any kind for broadcast over the radio, particularly since no way had yet been demonstrated to make money from such programming. Since RCA needed the programs to

Edwin Howard Armstrong (1890-1954)

sell its radios, Sarnoff urged the company to begin providing them as a public service. Although most of RCA's first shows were music broadcasts, Sarnoff demonstrated the potential of radio for bringing newsworthy events into the home when RCA broadcast a live description of the world heavyweight championship boxing match between Jack Dempsey and Georges Carpentier on July 2, 1921.

The public quickly proved Sarnoff's vision of the impact of radio to be correct. Sales of radios skyrocketed as more and more people sought access to the events, information, and entertainment that radio provided. In 1922, RCA's first full year of radio sales, the company's gross income (the total income before expenses) exceeded $11 million.

"During the fourth round of the fight, as Dempsey finished Carpentier off with a flurry of blows to the head, the heat inside the RCA transmitter shed had climbed to a dangerous level. Moments after Carpentier hit the canvas, the transmitter blew out completely. Had the fight gone another round, the broadcast would have been a total flop."
—Daniel Stashower, author of *The Boy Genius and the Mogul*

THE RADIO NETWORK

Sarnoff, however, realized that much of the interest was because of the novelty of radio. Once that wore off, he saw that the only way to keep customers and add new ones would be to steadily increase the number and quality of programs on the air. But programs cost money, and RCA could not afford to supply individual programming to many different radio stations. The idea of obtaining corporate sponsors who would pay for the broadcast in exchange for the goodwill and publicity such a gesture would generate had just started to catch on. But again, finding sponsors who could afford to pay for the programs broadcast by all these small radio stations was nearly impossible.

The RCA Radiola 60 floor model radio, 1929

Sarnoff, who had risen to the rank of general manager of RCA, recognized that the answer to the problems lay in creating a network made up of hundreds of stations that could all broadcast a program at once and share the expense. In September 1926, the National Broadcasting Company (NBC) was formed as a subsidiary company to create the network of stations he envisioned. The venture was so successful that just five months later, the company formed a second collection of radio stations. The

Chief engineer O.B. Hanson (standing) and technicians in the main control room as the first NBC radio show went on the air in 1926

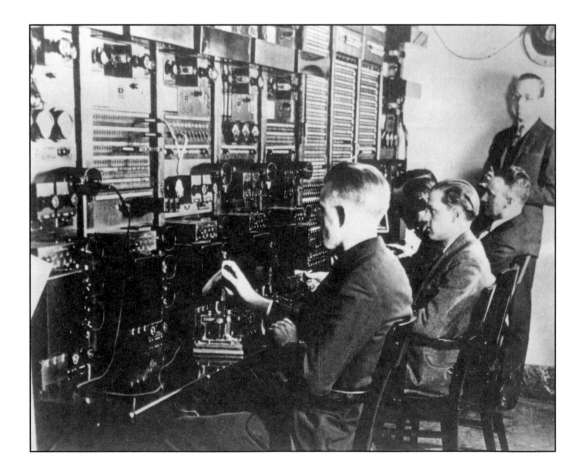

efficiency of the two networks, known as NBC Red and NBC Blue, allowed NBC to dominate the industry. The vastly improved programming they provided increased the demand for radios, and RCA became one of the most profitable corporations in the United States.

SARNOFF AT THE TOP

In 1930, Sarnoff was rewarded for his efforts by being named president of RCA. He was a most unlikely man to reign as the undisputed leader of the broadcast programming industry. Uncomfortable in the public light, Sarnoff preferred analyzing new developments in technology to dealing with the glamorous world of celebrity entertainers. Although he was a bold, decisive leader, he was also a loner who was insecure in his abilities. He was so suspicious of underlings who showed drive and initiative that he openly admitted, "I don't want anyone around as smart as I am."

A workaholic who rarely socialized, Sarnoff was an intimidating man to work for. He could be ruthless in his business dealings and became almost obsessed with monopolizing United States broadcasting. The hardhearted side of his nature was especially evident in his dealings with his friend Edwin Armstrong. Sarnoff encouraged Armstrong to work on a new, improved form of radio broadcasting known as FM. (All stations at the time used the AM form.) Then he suddenly opposed the development of the technology when he saw that it threatened to open up the broadcasting field to new

subsidiary: a company owned by another company

NBC grew to so dominate the American airwaves that in 1941 the Federal Communications Commission ordered the company to sell off its Blue division to competitors, who reorganized as the American Broadcasting Corporation (ABC) in 1945.

FM (frequency modulation): to encode a radio wave by varying its frequency

AM (amplitude modulation): to encode a radio wave by varying the amplitude (strength) of the wave

competitors. He used his considerable influence to get the FCC to put regulatory roadblocks in the way of Armstrong's superior technology, triggering a power struggle that ruined Armstrong's life. Sarnoff was partly speaking of himself when he noted, "Competition brings out the best in products and the worst in men."

Through his stubbornness, Sarnoff squandered much of his company's huge lead over his broadcasting competition by the end of the golden age of radio. Failing to recognize the power of celebrities in the new media age he had created, Sarnoff refused to pay large salaries to his top stars and as a result lost them to competitors. In one of the worst misjudgments in entertainment history, he let go his most popular star, comedian Jack Benny, in favor of comedian Horace Heidt. Heidt's show failed disastrously while Benny enjoyed ever increasing success at rival network Columbia Broadcasting System (CBS).

SIGHT ADDED TO SOUND

But while Sarnoff's skills in working with entertainers and employees were often suspect, he retained his uncanny knack for envisioning the future of broadcast technology. Even while radio was in its infancy, Sarnoff was already looking ahead to the next step. It was clear to him that if people could transmit sound over the airwaves, eventually they would be able to transmit visual images as well. As early as 1923, Sarnoff used the word "television," which he defined as "the technical name for seeing instead of hearing by radio."

The Sad Story of Edwin Armstrong

Few people have ever done as much for an industry as Edwin Howard Armstrong did for radio and received so little reward. Armstrong was born in New York City on December 18, 1890. He became fascinated with wireless technology and the work of Guglielmo Marconi while still in high school in Yonkers. His room was filled with electronic gear, including an audion tube. Invented by Lee de Forest in 1906, the audion was an improved version of the Fleming tube and it could detect radio signals. In 1913, while Armstrong was an engineering student at Columbia University, he devised a regenerative circuit to feed the electromagnetic waves from a radio transmission back through the audion tube again and again. This greatly amplified radio signals and allowed Armstrong to create what was then the most sensitive radio receiver in existence.

During World War I, Armstrong served in the U.S. armed force's signal corps. While enlisted, he invented the super-heterodyne circuit, a system that made it possible for radio receivers to be more selective, allowing the listener to tune in a single station more easily. Westinghouse bought the superheterodyne patent in 1920. This technology allowed them to start up the experimental KDKA station in Pittsburgh. Not long after, RCA bought all the radio patents owned by Westinghouse and some from other companies as well, including Armstrong's patent for regenera-tion. The income from these and other patents allowed Armstrong to work independently. But de Forest objected to Armstrong's regenerative circuit patent and began a costly and exhausting patent fight between the two inventors. Armstrong lost much money as well as pride when de Forest beat him in their court fight, an outcome that most industry historians regard as unjust.

Armstrong next developed a whole new type of radio transmission known as FM, for frequency modulation. FM offered superior sound quality and far less static interference from atmospheric conditions than AM radio. After spending most of the 1930s perfecting FM radio, Armstrong offered to sell his achievement to his old friend, David Sarnoff of RCA. Sarnoff, who controlled the AM markets and wanted no competition, rejected the deal—until he saw how well FM worked. RCA offered Armstrong $1 million for the patents. Armstrong, however, wanted royalties—a percentage of the profits made on his invention. Negotiations were set aside during World War II.

When the war ended, Armstrong found himself in another patent fight when RCA and others began using his FM technology. The legal battles depressed and exhausted Armstrong and hurt him financially. On January 31, 1954, the creator of FM technology now used by more than half the commercial radio stations in the United States committed suicide.

That same year, a Westinghouse engineer, Vladimir Zworykin, took out his first patent on a device that he called an iconoscope—the first step toward a crude system of transmitting pictures by radio waves. Sarnoff hired Zworykin in 1929 to develop television for RCA.

This time, though, Sarnoff did not have all the innovative technology under his control. In fact, Philo Farnsworth, an inventor working independently, had developed his own television system and had demonstrated it a year earlier than Zworykin's version. Farnsworth had a system ready for commercial use by 1930, well ahead of Zworykin. The Great Depression, however, stunted Farnsworth's effort until he could get financing from the

Philo Farnsworth called his camera tube an "image dissector" because it cut the image into lines and then reassembled it again, line by line. Farnsworth is shown here in 1938 with an improved version of his device.

Philadelphia Storage Battery Company (Philco) to market his televisions.

RCA fought back furiously, spending millions of dollars on research, challenging Farnsworth's patents in court, and finally negotiating with Farnsworth for use of his patents. (Farnsworth was the only inventor to prevail in a patent dispute with RCA.) Despite Sarnoff's best efforts, however, RCA failed to meet his expected timetable for the development of commercial television. By 1938 a few thousand television sets had been sold in the United States, primarily in New York, but they were of poor quality, and there were only a few dozen experimental stations providing any kind of programming. Finally, on April 20, 1939, RCA used the occasion of the New York World's Fair to demonstrate and promote its new television. "It is with a feeling of humbleness," declared Sarnoff, "that I come to this moment of announcing the birth in this country of a new art so important in its implications that it is bound to affect all society. It is an art which shines like a torch of hope in the troubled world. . . . Now we add sight to sound."

GENERAL SARNOFF AND THE WORLD SERIES

Accustomed to being far out in front of any competition, Sarnoff expected RCA to establish its technology so solidly as the industry standard that it would control the television market as it had the radio market. The plan sputtered, however, as NBC ran into a problem similar to that which had plagued it at the birth of network radio: lack of programs.

In 1928, General Electric started an experimental television station. The station made history by broadcasting the first televised drama, "The Queen's Messenger," to a very limited area, with the sound for the production being simultaneously broadcast over a radio station.

Zworykin and the Television

While much of television technology emerged in bits and pieces from a number of sources, the man who exercised the greatest influence over its development was Vladimir Kosma Zworykin. He was born on July 30, 1889, in Murom, Russia, near Moscow. Zworykin, the youngest of seven children in a well-to-do family, was fascinated by electricity and attended the University of St. Petersburg with the hope of studying physics. His father, however, insisted that he go into the more practical field of engineering. As a result, Zworykin transferred to the Institute of Technology in St. Petersburg. There he became a devoted student of Boris Rosing, a professor who had dreams of developing a system of electronic transmission of images.

Russia's entry into World War I interrupted his studies. Zworykin joined the army, where he was assigned to build a radio transmission station and then sent to a radio school for officers. But at the war's end, with the nation in turmoil due to the Communist revolution, Zworykin fled Russia. He gradually made his way to the United States, where he was employed by the Westinghouse electronics company.

While at Westinghouse, Zworykin continued working during his free time on his dream of television. He built on the work of others to create an iconoscope, which transmitted images. The iconoscope contained a small plate coated with light-sensitive material. A lens focused an object in front of the iconoscope tube, transferring the image to the metal coating in the form of varying electric charges. A beam of electrons could then scan the plate and change the stored charges into electrical impulses. A cathode-ray receiver could receive that signal and translate the waves back into electronic impulses that produced an image.

When Zworykin demonstrated his invention to Westinghouse management, however, the reception was so fuzzy that the executives told him to work on something more practical. Zworykin continued to work on the receiver, looking for ways to create a greater concentration of photo-electric dots that would give his system more sensitivity.

By 1929 he developed the kinescope, a receiver that could display clearly recognizable images. This attracted David Sarnoff's attention. When asked what it would take to have a product ready for the commercial market, Zworykin estimated two years and $100,000. He badly underestimated. Zworykin and RCA spent over $50 million before finally putting a product on the market in 1946, more than 13 years after Zworykin expected to be finished.

The inventor of television was perhaps the harshest critic of the way the broadcast business developed. Disappointed that television was not used primarily as an educational tool, Zworykin refused to watch the shows put on by the commercial networks. He thought of television as a way for people to see things their eyes couldn't reach, such as the U.S. space program's use of television to view the dark side of the moon. He continued working on improvements in color television before retiring in 1954.

Zworykin also worked on other visual technologies. In 1940, he hired a Canadian scientist, James Hillier, and the two of them built the first RCA electron microscope. The snooperscope and the sniperscope, two important military tools used during World War II, were developed from his research on infrared image tubes. Altogether, Zworykin held more than 120 U.S. patents and more than two dozen awards, including the National Medal of Science. But he is remembered as the father of television. By the time of his death on July 29, 1982—one day short of his 93rd birthday—more than 500 million televisions were in use throughout the world.

Zworykin's iconoscope had a mechanism that strengthened the image signal by storing the light energy it received.

37

David Sarnoff standing before television cameras at the New York World's Fair in 1939

Without programs, consumers had no use for televisions. RCA sold fewer than 3,000 television sets in 1939, drastically short of the 100,000 the company had projected. Furthermore, setting up television studios proved to be a difficult and expensive proposition. Having poured millions of dollars into television research, RCA had virtually nothing to show for it at the beginning of the 1940s. NBC did not get its first station, WNBT, up and running until 1941, and even then it could manage only two hours of programming a day.

World War II then brought the new industry to a standstill as all research money was channeled into military areas. Sarnoff himself volunteered his services to the U.S. in the area of communications. Sarnoff coordinated radio communications for the D-day invasion, selecting the site for broadcasting and buying all the necessary equipment. In gratitude, General Dwight Eisenhower named him a brigadier general in the U.S. Army Signal Corps. Sarnoff returned from the war in 1945 with his new title (he insisted that all employees address him as "General") and a renewed interest in making commercial network television work. His efforts would be backed by record revenues from RCA's war contracts.

NBC finally turned the corner in 1947, thanks largely to its coverage of the World Series, which attracted nearly four million viewers. At that point, television quickly usurped radio's role as the family center of communications. But Sarnoff was not finished with shaping the world of broadcasting. There was still the matter of color television.

Uncharacteristically, Sarnoff was caught napping by rival CBS in early color TV technology. But during the 1950s he led a massive research effort to create an electronic color system that proved far superior to CBS's. Again Sarnoff's RCA leaped out in front of its rivals in developing the technology that became the industry standard.

David Sarnoff, who had been named president of RCA in 1930, held that position until his retirement in 1970. He died on December 12, 1971, at the age of 80.

An early television studio at NBC

LEGACY

David Sarnoff was a serious, impersonal figure working in a glamorous industry. Obsessed with the technological side of the business, he spent little time improving the value of the programming. He expressed idealistic ideas in statements such as, "The ultimate contribution of television will be its service toward the unification of the life of the nation, and, at the same time, the greater development of the life of the individual," and spoke of television as "a creative force we must learn to utilize for the benefit of all mankind." Yet he took no responsibility for the quality of what his own network put on the air; he regarded many programs as questionable at best.

Nonetheless, Sarnoff was the most influential figure in the birth of broadcasting. He was directly in the middle of development processes that created radio, television, and color television technology. He envisioned a future for commercial radio and then brought that vision to reality. He virtually invented network broadcasting, and he created the network that dominated commercial radio through most of its glory years. In fact, he started not one but two of the major television networks, since the NBC Blue Division later became the American Broadcasting Company (ABC). A visionary to the end, Sarnoff in his later years pioneered the made-for-TV movie and predicted the invention of the videocassette recorder (VCR).

During his career, David Sarnoff ushered in one of the most significant changes in modern society. Building upon his pioneering efforts, television has become a worldwide phenomenon. In the early twenty-first century, it was estimated that the average American family spends about 50 hours per week in front of the television.

> "Sarnoff's channel was always dialed to the future."
> —Marcy Carsey and Tom Werner, *Time*

VCR (videocassette recorder): an electronic device for recording video images and sound on a videotape. Once the images have been recorded, the VCR can play the tape on a television screen.

2

WILLIAM PALEY

THE MASTER SALESMAN AT CBS

Unlike David Sarnoff, upon whose heels he followed, William Paley had little knowledge of or interest in the technical aspects of radios and televisions, nor did he have his rival's vision for the future of the industry. Paley, in fact, did not recognize the potential of television at first and switched his emphasis from radio to television tardily and reluctantly. Yet historians rank him with Sarnoff as the two most influential business builders in the broadcasting industry. The *New York Times* went so far as to say that Paley "is to American broadcasting as Carnegie was to steel, Ford to the automobile, Luce to publishing, and Ruth to baseball."

Paley's gift was in sales. He had a knack for understanding what his customers, the American

William Samuel Paley (1901-1990) was a whiz at programming and sales, but he also set a high standard for news programs broadcast on CBS. "This medium has to absolutely live on the basis of fairness and balance or else we're lost," he said.

public, wanted to hear over the radio and see on television. By aiming his programs at the masses and organizing an innovative network system of affiliates and advertising sponsors, Paley found a way to make television immensely profitable as well as popular. As a result, his Columbia Broadcasting System (CBS) eventually surpassed NBC as the most influential television network in the 1950s and 1960s.

THE FAMILY CIGAR BUSINESS

William Samuel Paley, the son of Goldie Drell Paley and Samuel Paley, was born on September 28, 1901, in Chicago, Illinois. His grandfather, Isaac Paley, had operated a prosperous lumber business in the Ukraine near Kiev before moving the family to Chicago in 1890. After Isaac lost much of their fortune through bad stock investments, Sam supported the family by rolling and selling cigars. He hired others to help him and eventually established the Congress Cigar Company.

As a young boy, Bill Paley proved to be a good student when motivated; his main interests lay in music and reading. He showed enough talent as a pianist to consider a career in that field, but he eventually grew tired of the constant practicing it required. Eager to please his father, he spent much of his spare time working at the cigar factory, sweeping floors and running errands.

At the age of 16, Bill was sent to the Western Military Academy in Alton, Illinois, where he applied himself so intensely to his studies that he received two years' worth of credits in one year. That enabled

stock: shares of ownership of a corporation

him to enroll at the University of Chicago in 1918 at the age of 17. Shortly after he began there, however, his father reached the end of his patience with frequent strikes by his plant workers. In 1919, he relocated the company to Philadelphia, Pennsylvania. Bill went along with the family and enrolled at the prestigious Wharton School of Business at the University of Pennsylvania. There he decided to devote his career to the family business, a decision of which his father heartily approved. Bill spent summers working at the Congress Cigar Company, learning all facets of the business in preparation for taking charge of it some day. Meanwhile, the company expanded to include 12 factories in Pennsylvania, Delaware, and New Jersey.

Shortly after graduating in 1922, Bill was made a vice president of the company. One of his duties in this position involved overseeing the company's advertising. Bill became intrigued with the emerging phenomenon of radio broadcasting. At the time, radios were so scarce that he was unable to purchase one and had to have a radio custom-made for him. He soon made a habit of listening to the radio until late at night. While doing so, he concluded that if the popularity of radio continued to grow, radio advertising could reach a far greater number of potential customers than ads in newspapers and magazines.

RADIO: A NEW WAY TO SELL CIGARS

During the summer of 1925, Sam Paley and his brother Jake went away on a business trip, leaving

Bill in charge of the cigar company. Bill decided to put his hunch about radio advertising to the test. He agreed to pay $50 per show to sponsor the *La Palina Hour* (named after one of the company's cigar brands) on radio station WCAU in Philadelphia. The show featured a singer accompanied by a ten-piece orchestra. Upon their return, Bill's father and uncle were outraged at the waste of money and ordered him to pull out of radio. His uncle Jake told him, "That's nonsense; that machine is never going to work."

Sam Paley, however, discovered what a huge impact the radio advertising had made when people kept asking why he stopped sponsoring the show. Noting that the $50 spent on the radio show was gathering more publicity than the one-half million dollars per year the company spent on print ads, he had a change of heart. He gave Bill the task of producing the company's weekly 30-minute radio program. Bill began arranging for singers, orchestras, and comedians to appear on the broadcasts.

While Bill Paley was gaining experience in the radio business, an unexpected opportunity fell into his lap. It all began with a music agent named Arthur Judson. Seeing the need for radio programming, Judson had tried to create a performers' bureau that could provide entertainment for radio broadcasts for a fee. When David Sarnoff at NBC took no interest in the project, Judson formed his own broadcasting network in 1926, the United Independent Broadcasters network. Lacking the financial resources to keep the project afloat, Judson

Although he failed to succeed in the broadcasting business, Arthur Judson was influential in the music world. He went on to manage both the New York Philharmonic and the Philadelphia Orchestra, as well as many famous musicians such as opera singer Mario Lanza.

sold controlling interest in the company to the Columbia Phonograph Company in 1927. Columbia, which produced and sold phonograph records, was eager to compete against NBC and RCA. The network went on the air in September of that year but lost so much money that it was in danger of going out of business before the year was over.

In desperation, one of Judson's partners, Jerome Louchheim, approached Sam Paley about buying the network. Louchheim knew Paley was both wealthy and interested in broadcasting. "You at least have a cigar to advertise and you can make some use of it," he argued. Sam had no desire to get into the broadcasting business, but Bill did. His father had just sold Congress Cigar for nearly $30 million, so Bill had some ready cash and was willing to risk $500,000 of the family fortune to buy 50.3 percent of what was now called the Columbia Broadcasting System (CBS)—but only with his father's support. Sam Paley gave his blessing, and on September 19, 1928, Bill Paley found himself in charge of a radio network. His intent was to get the company's affairs organized and then return to his duties at the cigar company, where he still worked as an executive.

GIVING THE PUBLIC WHAT IT WANTS

When Paley first appeared at Columbia's offices, the employees would not believe that this young man, just days away from his 27th birthday, was their boss. Paley, meanwhile, wondered what he had gotten himself into. The company's management was in chaos. CBS owned few assets with which to

"Paley was no doubt excited when he arrived. . . . But his reception was something less than he had hoped for. A stocky office boy refused to admit the boyish-looking president, demanding to see credentials and to know the purpose of his visit."
—Lewis J. Paper, author of *Empire: William S. Paley and the Making of CBS*

challenge the industry giant, NBC, whose programming efforts were backed by the huge profits of its parent company, radio-manufacturer RCA. CBS lacked radio equipment of its own to sell; to make matters worse, it had to use RCA equipment to broadcast its programs. CBS owned no stations, it was nothing more than a loose affiliation of 16 independent radio stations. It seemed unlikely that tiny CBS could possibly compete.

Paley applied his sales expertise to the problem. He heeded his father's advice to hire the smartest, most talented people he could find and listen to them. This was especially important for Paley, as he had virtually no understanding of the technology involved in putting programs on the air. Peter Goldmark, one of CBS's top technical experts, once said of Paley, "He has seldom given a talk on communications or seemed fully to understand how communications technology was changing the modern world and what to do about it." His primary focus was simply on making his company profitable.

What Paley did possess was a unique understanding of what the public wanted. His approach to the radio business crystallized when he observed two movie theaters on the same street. One of the theaters was lavishly decorated and offered more comforts and amenities than its shabby neighbor. Yet Paley noted that customers attended the theater that had the movie they wanted to see, regardless of the facilities. From this he concluded that technological advances in radio were not nearly as important as the programming. He would concede

NBC and RCA their huge lead in the equipment but would compete with them for the programming.

After observing the popularity of NBC's *Amos 'n' Andy* comedy show in 1929, Paley made the decision to offer light entertainment rather than serious or fine arts programming. While NBC initially aired a wide variety of offerings such as classical music, lectures, and educational programs in addition to its comedy shows, CBS focused on light comedy and drama, and popular music. In 1930, Paley helped bring about a merger of several of the leading concert bureaus—agencies that negotiated contracts for

Freeman Gosden (left) and Charles Correll perform as Amos and Andy in the NBC radio studios, before they switched to CBS. Their comedy was on the radio for almost 30 years. Gosden and Correll were white; their characters were African Americans. In the television version of the show, which aired on CBS from 1951-1953, the characters were played by black actors.

performing artists—to form the Columbia Concerts Corporation. This gave CBS access to 125 of the most talented concert performers in the nation.

PALEY THE SALESMAN

Paley's sales skills proved especially valuable in lining up programming talent. When he approached popular conductor Paul Whiteman about doing a radio show, Whiteman told him that he had no interest in doing anything with radio. Paley kept after him, finally zeroing in on the fact that in doing a radio broadcast Whiteman could perform for an audience far larger than at any concert hall. He finally persuaded Whiteman, thus locking up his first major entertainment personality. Similarly, nationally known humorist Will Rogers initially refused to do a radio show because he could not imagine performing without the benefit of an audience to react to what he was doing. Paley won him over by promising him a live studio audience. Paley then corralled more than three dozen company employees to sit in the studio as the audience while Rogers performed.

Trying to catch up with the head start enjoyed by NBC proved costly, and CBS struggled to survive during Paley's first year. Only with an influx of cash from the family coffers was he barely able to keep ahead of creditors. By early 1929, CBS had expanded to 49 stations in 42 locations, but it was still able to offer only 21 hours a week of network programming. In the spring of 1929, Paley was so strapped for funds that he entertained an offer from Adolph Zukor, head of the entertainment company

Paramount, to buy half the company for $4.5 million. Despite his weak position, Bill Paley stunned business experts by rejecting what appeared to be an incredibly generous offer. His move proved a shrewd one, however; Zukor upped the offer to $5 million, which gave CBS the funds to survive the difficult early years. Paley remained head of CBS and later bought the stock back from Zukor.

Adolph Zukor (1873-1976, at left) and Jesse Lasky, one of his early business partners, look over a Hollywood construction site. In 1912, Zukor screened the first feature-length film, Queen Elizabeth. *He went on to head Paramount Pictures.*

Zukor's investment and Paley's sales expertise helped CBS turn its fortunes around. He saw immediately that the key to making a radio network profitable was the sponsorship of advertisers. But when he started at CBS, only one out of five of the network's small stable of programs had a paying sponsor. Paley realized that unless he could find sponsors to pay for programming, he could neither attract performers nor keep his business afloat. To help with this problem, he hired an experienced public relations director to make his network known throughout the country. He then came up with a novel way both to make money and to provide incentive for radio stations to join and stay with his network. Unlike NBC, which made money by charging affiliated local stations up to $90 an hour to broadcast its programs, Paley gave his network programs to affiliates free of charge. In exchange, he required only that local stations agree to broadcast CBS-sponsored programs whenever he required it. Local stations were thrilled to get free programming, while advertisers loved Paley's system because it guaranteed them a wide audience for any network programming they chose to sponsor.

A prime example of William Paley's skill as a salesman involved George W. Hill, president of the American Tobacco Company. Paley was wooing Hill to sign on as a network sponsor, but he soon saw that Hill was stubborn about wanting to do things his own way. Paley then mentioned to Hill that CBS was planning a program of military marching music but that it was probably the wrong type of program for American Tobacco. Hill took the bait and decided that this was exactly what his company should sponsor. Before long, William Paley had negotiated a profitable deal with an influential sponsor to back 15 minutes of martial music five times a week.

SURGE TO PROFITABILITY

Under Paley's leadership, CBS surged to profitability almost overnight. The network earned nearly $500,000 in 1929 despite the terrible economic depression the nation was experiencing. In July of that year, he moved the company from its four-room office in the Paramount Tower into six spacious floors at Madison Avenue and 52nd Street. In December, he bought station WABC in New York for $390,000 to serve as his company's lead station.

Paley's business plan was to expand quickly while the radio broadcast business was still relatively disorganized. With Paley's enticing offer of free programming to affiliate stations, CBS was able to sign on affiliates more quickly than its giant rival, NBC. By 1931 it had more than 90 affiliates. Although the nation's economy was mired deep in the Great Depression, CBS cashed in on the explosive growth of interest in radio. In 1932, with the national audience estimated at more than 50 million people, CBS had no trouble selling program sponsorship and recorded an astounding $3 million profit. Total sales for the company jumped from $4.1 million in 1929 to $12.9 million in 1935.

CBS and the Evening News

The emphasis of early commercial radio and television was on light entertainment, although most stations also tried to provide some news for their listeners. Basically, these early news shows consisted of a person reading copy collected from various sources such as newspapers and wire services. (Wire services were agencies that hired reporters to provide timely news reports via telegraph that could be sold to media outlets such as newspapers.)

William Paley of CBS, however, saw news as an opportunity to create a positive image for his network. By 1930, he was hiring a separate staff to write and broadcast the news. This caused newspapers to view radio as a threat to their livelihood. The newspapers pressured the wire services to withhold their reports from radio, and, in 1933, the wire services complied. CBS responded by creating its own full-fledged news operation that included journalists gathering news, not just reading reports on the air. Under the leadership of Ed Klauber, CBS News developed so rapidly that by 1936 it had gained a reputation as a leader in covering worldwide events. Paley added to the professionalism of the news department by insisting that his reporters remain impartial in their news reports, and that only CBS News staff could write or broadcast the news.

In 1937, Klauber sent reporter Edward Murrow to Europe. There Murrow hired foreign correspondent William Shirer. The next year the two men provided CBS with eyewitness descriptions of Nazi Germany's takeover of Austria. Paley and the news department recognized the impact that this could have, and the network quickly put together a half-hour news special with the correspondents reporting live and on

Edward R. Murrow (1908-1965) writing one of his news reports during World War II.

Walter Cronkite (b. 1916) anchored the CBS Evening News *from 1962 to 1981 and gained a reputation as the most trusted figure in the United States because of his objective approach to the news.*

location. This special was the first *World News Roundup*, a program that evolved into a regular, daily 30-minute radio broadcast. "Columbia's coverage of the European crisis is superior to its competitors," William Paley later wired to Murrow, "and probably the best job ever done in radio broadcasting."

The reports from Murrow and the talented team of reporters he assembled kept Americans informed as war broke out across Europe. Murrow was acclaimed for his daring—he once broadcast from a rooftop in London as German bombs fell—as well as his integrity. CBS News became widely respected for its high journalistic standards.

As television emerged as the successor to radio in the late 1940s and early 1950s, CBS transferred its reputation for quality to the visual medium. Well into the 1960s, the network poured money and effort into its television news organization.

The CBS Evening News lost its edge over the competition in the 1970s, along with the rest of the network's programming. But the half-hour daily news show CBS pioneered was copied by all the major networks and became the primary source of world news for millions of people.

In a *Fortune* magazine article published in June 1935, Paley's associates described him in glowing terms. "Not only is he a master advertiser and feeler of the public pulse," reported the article, "but these gentlemen say he is the greatest organizer, the best executive, the quickest thinker, the coolest negotiator they have ever seen."

Paley loved the show-business side of his work, and he showed a unique gift for evaluating talent. Perhaps his most remarkable coup occurred in June 1931. While sailing to Europe on a business trip, he heard a song called "I Surrender Dear," by an unknown artist. Convinced that he had discovered a major talent, he found out the singer's name and then sent a cable back to his subordinates, telling them to sign the man to a contract. The singer was Bing Crosby, who turned out to be one of the most successful popular entertainers of all time.

At the same time, Paley was not above raiding talent from his rivals at NBC. In the early days of CBS, he lured away such NBC stars as Al Jolson and Eddie Cantor and even outbid his rival for the Lux Radio Theater, one of NBC's most popular shows. Determined to end NBC's long-standing reign as the most popular radio network, Paley lured NBC's top comedy stars—Jack Benny, Red Skelton, Burns and Allen, and Edgar Bergen—to CBS in the late 1940s by offering them huge salary increases.

Harry Lillis "Bing" Crosby (1903-1977) was a respected actor as well as a singer. He made dozens of movies (many of them musicals) from the 1930s through the 1960s. He won an Academy Award for Best Actor for his performance in the 1944 film Going My Way.

UNDERESTIMATING TELEVISION

The one area of mass entertainment where Paley's crystal ball failed him initially was in the area of

television. As early as June 1931, his CBS company had begun looking into the possibilities of television broadcasting, but Paley was not interested in technological innovation, only in running a profitable company. He thought television would hurt radio and didn't see any profit in it.

William Paley (left) loved socializing with stars, such as the popular husband-and-wife comedy team Gracie Allen and George Burns, pictured here in 1952.

CBS did some sporadic experimental work in television broadcasting. In 1941, its experimental station made an attempt at television programming, airing a show in which a mother read a fairy tale to her child. But Paley was unable to detect what NBC's Sarnoff saw: the eventual conversion of the huge national radio audience to television.

Paley's dismissal of television as an expensive, high-risk venture led him to close down the CBS experimental station even as NBC was forging ahead. He focused all of his efforts on his lifelong goal of overtaking NBC as the most listened-to radio network in the nation. But then in 1947, NBC televised the World Series baseball games, which attracted an estimated audience of 3.9 million viewers, nearly 3.5 million of those viewers watching in bars. Those audience figures jolted Paley into realizing that he had misjudged the situation.

Ironically, his obsession with overtaking NBC as the radio leader proved to be a huge windfall for him in the television wars. His talent raids on NBC in the late 1940s were intended to boost CBS's radio audience numbers. But when he suddenly needed television programming, top comedians such as Jack Benny and Red Skelton proved to be as popular in the new medium as they had been on radio. The boost from these stars, combined with Paley's knack for developing programs that mass audiences would watch, allowed CBS to surpass NBC in the 1950s as the most popular television network. By 1954, television was a runaway success with over 32 million sets in use in the United States. As the network

with the most viewers, CBS could command the highest advertising prices and became the largest single seller of advertising in the world.

Realizing that he had avoided disaster from his miscalculation of TV's place in society only by blind luck, Paley vowed not to make the same mistake twice. Wisely recognizing that color television was

By the early 1950s, television—like baseball—had become part of American life.

Peter Goldmark (1906-1977) was a pioneer in color television. Here Goldmark (left) sketches a television transmission diagram in 1937 for Gilbert Seldes of CBS.

the next step in broadcasting evolution, Paley poured a great deal of money and effort into making CBS the first network to use such television technology. This time he erred on the side of too much investment. CBS spent more than $60 million on color television research and development only to produce technology far inferior to that developed by NBC, which became the industry standard.

Paley, however, was so far ahead of the competition in understanding what programming would be popular that he was able to overcome such missteps. Unlike Sarnoff, who had no interest in television shows and seldom watched them, Paley enjoyed the programs his network put on. Keeping the focus on the kind of light entertainment he enjoyed, CBS reigned for nearly three decades as the dominant force in television.

"YOU CAN NEVER ENJOY SUCCESS"

During that time, Paley ran CBS with a loose rein, setting the general course for the company but rarely issuing specific orders and frequently letting others run the show during his long absences. He enjoyed the privileges that came with his position; while visiting studios in Los Angeles, for example, he had an aide assigned to follow him wherever he went, carrying a chair. Whenever Paley decided to sit, he did so, expecting the aide to have the chair in place. Despite his enormous success, he fretted constantly over his business. "The nervous strain is terrible because you can never settle down to enjoy success," he once admitted. "It's over too quickly and forgotten." Paley admitted to being a difficult person to know, and his friend Irene Selznick once remarked, "Bill Paley is so contradictory, you don't see the same fella twice." Indeed, he had a wide reputation as a party-goer, yet he jealously guarded his privacy. He was often criticized for insensitivity, yet praised for his charm.

Paley made several attempts to retire from the company, but kept returning to active roles when he was dissatisfied with the performances of his successors. In his last years, his fears that CBS would slip came true as the network was overtaken by more innovative programming efforts at rivals NBC and ABC. Paley's active involvement gradually diminished in the the 1980s, but he remained involved in the company until his death in 1990 at the age of 89. Ten years later, CBS merged with Viacom, Inc., the world's largest media company. Viacom's well-known companies include United Paramount Network (UPN), Black Entertainment Television (BET), Showtime Networks Inc. (SNI), Paramount Television (which includes the *Star Trek* franchise), Paramount Pictures, Blockbuster video stores, and book publisher Simon & Schuster.

LEGACY

In the words of biographer David Halberstam, William Paley "was for 50 years the supreme figure of modern broadcasting, first in radio, then in television." It was Paley who determined the course of network broadcasting by building CBS into a profitable business through the use of light entertainment shows geared at a mass audience and taking advantage of the advertising dollars such a mass audience could generate. In so doing, he revolutionized the American economy by making the home the primary marketplace where goods and services are sold. Paley's aggressive use of television as a sales vehicle, with the vast majority of programs being broadcast from a single powerful centralized command center through a huge national network of affiliates, solidified that system as the form that U.S. television broadcasting would take over the next 30 years.

Equally significant was Paley's influence on American culture. He was largely responsible for determining the kinds of programs that network television decided to broadcast and that American families watched in their homes. Even before the advent of television, American broadcasting had stopped serving as a medium for education and fine arts in favor of mass market entertainment and commercialism. Although CBS billed itself as the champion of quality television programming, and Paley never saw a need to apologize for what he put on the air, historians cite CBS as the main influence in continuing that trend in television.

3

GERALD LEVIN

HBO: THE FIRST CABLE CHANNEL

Gerald Levin always seemed out of place in the flash and glitter world of high-profile electronic media. Nothing about his appearance or demeanor distinguished him as anything more than just a guy in a suit performing some valuable but anonymous management function. But beneath that quiet surface beat the heart of a swashbuckling gambler. Levin's willingness to take risks earned him praise as a genius with remarkable insight into the future as well as criticism as a bumbler who had no clue what he was doing.

Levin carved a new future for electronic media by betting his company's survival on a totally untested method of distributing its broadcast signal—through cable connections rather than through the airwaves.

Gerald Levin (b. 1939) solved a distribution problem, creating the first national cable television channel, Home Box Office. He went on to head the media company Time Warner.

The stunning success of his Home Box Office channel broke the stranglehold that the major broadcast networks had held on television since its inception. Building on that success, Levin eventually took control of the media giant Time Warner, and then risked that company's reputation and financial stability on a breathtaking gamble to combine electronic and print media with the new wave of the Internet. Like all gamblers, Levin found that luck is a fickle friend.

Internet: an international network that allows computers to exchange information

A SERIOUS STUDENT

Gerald Manuel Levin was born on May 6, 1939, in Philadelphia, Pennsylvania. His parents were both children of Jewish immigrants who had fled persecution in Eastern Europe. His father operated a butter and egg business while his mother taught piano. Their incomes provided a comfortable living for them in their suburban Philadelphia home. Gerald was a bright and talented boy with poise beyond his years. When he was only nine years old, a cantor failed to appear for a service at the local synagogue. Gerald knew enough Hebrew to perform the cantor's duties. He won a public speaking contest when he was in junior high and often played the lead role in high school plays. Gerald was noted for his memory, especially when it came to facts regarding two of his greatest interests, the Philadelphia Athletics baseball team and Oscar-winning motion pictures.

Gerald Levin attended Haverford College in Pennsylvania, where he earned a reputation for strict personal discipline as well as academic ability.

According to one of his roommates, Brownlow Speer, he "was very jolly and gregarious for at least part of the day. But at eight P.M. or so he'd start studying and you wouldn't see him." Levin did find time, however, to date Carol Needleman, whom he married in 1959.

While at school, Levin studied biblical literature, with the intention of becoming a rabbi. He was particularly fascinated by what he called "the continuity between the Judaic and Christian traditions." In the course of his studies, however, he began to question his strict Jewish upbringing. "I made a complete transformation through college," he said, "coming out very spiritual but areligious." When he graduated in 1960 as the valedictorian of his class at Haverford, he refused all honors and burned his college papers to make a statement that the effort put into the studies was what really mattered.

Lawyer

Gerald Levin then attended graduate school at the University of Pennsylvania, where he obtained a law degree in 1963. He spent four years practicing law with the firm of Simpson, Thatcher and Bartlett before making another career change in 1967. This time he took a position as general manager and chief operations officer of a small business consulting company called Development and Resources Corporation.

Following his divorce from his wife in 1970, Levin took a new job, traveling halfway around the world to work as a representative for International

Basic Economics Corporation in Tehran, Iran. Two years later, he returned home and began working as a vice president of programming for the company's new cable television operations, Home Box Office (HBO), a newly formed subsidiary of communications giant Time, Inc. HBO was trying to find a market niche airing sports programming, motion pictures that had just finished showing in movie theaters, and some low-budget original specials to cable viewers in Pennsylvania and New Jersey for a monthly fee.

LEVIN AND THE SATELLITE

Cable television had been in existence since the early days of commercial television, but on a tiny scale compared to the national networks. Most cable stations were struggling to survive, and few entertainment industry executives saw much future in pay-per-view television. The idea of making a profit by charging viewers to watch television programs seemed highly doubtful given the fact that the major networks, because of advertising revenue, were able to provide programming free of charge. Network television simply broadcast over the airwaves, while cable television required the creation of an expensive and elaborate system of cable connections. Programming was often delivered to the stations in the form of videocassettes, one to each station airing a program. Other alternatives were being attempted; HBO, for example, was working with microwave technology to distribute the programming to its cable subscribers but that had proved difficult even in

revenue: the amount of money collected by a business

its limited distribution area. Until the early 1970s, the only type of pay television that had shown any potential for sales were single, highly publicized events—such as heavyweight championship boxing matches—that could charge huge fees to support the cost of providing the programming.

Looking for new ways to distribute programs, Levin was drawn to the idea of satellite technology. RCA owned a communications satellite called Satcom I that orbited Earth at a height of about 22,000 miles. It was capable of relaying programs to stations throughout the world, instantly solving HBO's distribution problems.

Negotiating a fee with RCA for use of its satellite and ironing out some of the technical difficulties

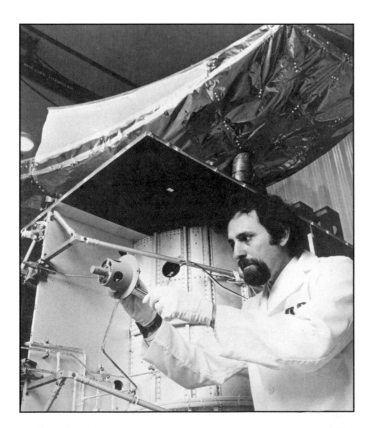

An RCA engineer adjusts a thruster on the Satcom communication satellite shortly before it was launched into space in 1975.

Communications satellites like RCA's are basically orbiting antennas that receive television signals from Earth and then rebroadcast them over an area thousands of miles wide. A television signal makes the 44,000-mile trip in less than a fifth of a second. Because the signal travels vertically through the atmosphere, there is little interference from the weather and reception is almost always clear. Even in 1975, satellite transmission was less expensive than other methods.

Communication satellites orbit about 22,000 miles above the Earth's equator. At this altitude, a satellite must complete a full circle around the earth every 24 hours in order to stay aloft. Given the rotation of Earth, that altitude keeps the satellite in the same relative position. This is called a "geosynchronous orbit." In 2005, several hundred satellites were in geosynchronous orbit, providing telephone and data communications. Television, however, was the largest user of communication satellites.

would be far too expensive for a company with a tiny, two-state viewing area. But Levin saw that the satellite would instantly give HBO access to markets across the country. He was willing to gamble that if HBO organized and managed the process wisely, the huge increase in viewership would easily pay for any expense and allow for a solid profit.

Under Levin's direction, HBO began satellite transmission of programming in the spring of 1975. The results were so spectacular that industry experts wondered why no one had seen the potential before. By the end of 1977, HBO had signed up a million subscribers nationwide and was already beginning to turn a profit. The company's success spawned a host of imitators. By the end of 1979 the cable television business had captured the interest of viewers; 14.5 million of the nation's 78 million televisions were wired to receive cable television, and the industry was raking in nearly $1.5 billion in revenue. Building on the head start that Levin's gamble had provided, HBO dominated the industry, controlling nearly 80 percent of the business. The company continued to grow at an astounding pace, surpassing 3 million paying customers by the close of 1979.

MOVING UP THE CORPORATE LADDER

Gerald Levin was hailed as a business genius and his employers rewarded him well for his foresight. In 1976, he was promoted to president and chief executive officer of HBO. He then began moving up the corporate ladder within Time, advancing to the

position of vice president in charge of all of the company's cable television operations in 1979.

As a manager, Levin preached three main values: openness, creativity, and diversity. He dismissed those who worried that the cable stations offered so many choices that the marketplace would divide into too many pieces for any one to remain profitable. "The human desire for images and information, for songs and stories, is boundless," he proclaimed. "When was the last time consumers rejected more choice?"

Gerald Levin demonstrates the new cable channel HBO during its early days.

Origins of Cable Television

Cable television transmits images to television sets through coaxial cables. (Coaxial cable has an outer metal tube enclosing the central conducting core.) Cable systems receive television signals from a common antenna or satellite dish, then send the programs to individual subscribers. Cable developed in the late 1940s out of frustration with the lack of reception in remote or mountainous areas. It is unclear exactly who first came up with the idea of using cables to transfer television signals pulled in by antenna. The earliest documented instance is cited in a Tuckerman, Arkansas, newspaper report of November 18, 1948. The report describes the work of local appliance dealer Jim Y. Davidson in that town. Reception from the nearest station in Memphis, Tennessee, was so weak that Davidson was having difficulty selling television sets. He mounted a 100-foot antenna on the roof of a tall building and ran wires from it to television sets in his showroom, to one in the American Legion Hall, and to a private home.

Another television salesman, John Walson (1915-1993), experienced the same problems with poor reception in his home town of Mahanoy City, Pennsylvania, which was located in a valley between mountains that blocked television signals from Philadelphia. Walson erected an antenna atop a large utility pole at the peak of a mountain and relayed the signals to his store via wire. He soon switched to coaxial cable to improve reception. Walson said he started his cable transmissions in June 1948, before Davidson, but a warehouse fire wiped out his records.

In 1950, there were 70 cable systems serving 14,000 subscribers. Cable operators soon realized that they could provide more than clearer reception. They could also offer more choice of programs to viewers in a particular area by drawing in

A satellite dish used to transmit television programs

On behalf of The Cable Center, Stan Searle (left) presented the cable television pioneer award to John Walson in 1967.

a variety of distant signals. Local stations viewed this practice as unfair competition. Their concerns led the FCC to restrict long-distance transfer of signals into a particular area. Because of this restriction, cable grew slowly.

In 1962, there were roughly 800 distributors of cable television in the United States serving 850,000 subscribers. Restrictions against the cable industry eased in the early 1970s. At the same time, satellite communications gave cable companies a better way to send their transmissions, and cable enjoyed a surge of popularity. The 1984 Cable Act deregulated the industry. In the eight years that followed, cable companies spent $15 billion installing cable systems across the nation. As of 2004, more than 9,000 cable systems provided service to more than 73 million homes. The average cable subscriber received 40 channels, a vast increase over the 3 or 4 available before the arrival of cable.

During the 1980s, however, some industry analysts began to wonder if Levin was merely a mediocre manager who had lucked out on his satellite gamble. Indeed, some of Levin's decisions during the early part of that decade proved disastrous. He initiated a project called Teletext, a service designed to deliver news on demand to television stations via cable, which lost $35 million. Other plans of his to create new subscription television markets were estimated to have lost $100 million. Furthermore, he entered into a motion picture deal with TriStar Pictures, without placing any caps on the amount of money Time had to spend on making the movies. That left no incentive for the motion picture production people to hold down their costs. Their projects frequently ran well over budget, leaving Time stuck paying one-third of all the bills.

When Levin waged battle with Nicholas J. Nicholas Jr. to take over as CEO of Time in the mid-1980s, these missteps hurt him badly. When Nicholas prevailed, it seemed that Levin's brief time as a force in the communications business had come to an end. Levin felt frustrated and helpless, yet he remained sure that he was still the best person to lead the company. "I had a sense of mission about Time, Inc.," he said. "I believed with a kind of messianic zeal that I could figure out what it needed."

By creating a solid work record as an executive vice president and later vice chairman and director, Levin reestablished himself as a company leader. During the 1989 merger negotiations between Time, Inc., and Warner Communications, another major player in the industry, Levin performed an invaluable service for Time chairman J. Richard Munroe. When negotiations became complex and Time's management was undecided about how to proceed, Levin stepped in. He wrote most of Time's proposal, which helped complete the merger and the formation of Time Warner, Inc. Gerald Levin found the experience with high-stakes management exhilarating. "I realized I had another facet to my complex personality," he said, "and it had to do with being steely in the face of pressure."

CONTROL OF THE COMPANY

His confidence bolstered, Levin set about to assume control of the company. Displaying a toughness that surprised even his colleagues, Levin worked quietly behind the scenes with allies in the company to force the ouster of board chairman Nicholas in 1991. A year later, Levin moved just as decisively to force the resignation of nine board members who opposed his policies. His actions cleared the way for him to take over as chairman of Time Warner, the world's largest company in the field of journalism and creative and entertainment media, in 1993. Its assets included *Time* and *Sports Illustrated* magazines, Time-Life books, Warner Brothers motion picture and television productions, and the largest record company in the nation, Warner Music Group.

Levin's goal was to make the company even bigger and more modern. Few observers, however, thought he was up to the task of maintaining the strong tradition of Time Warner, much less building

Covers from two of the almost three dozen periodicals owned by Time Warner. The company began in 1923 with the publication of its first issue of Time *magazine.*

on it. Articles that appeared in such influential magazines as *The New Yorker* portrayed Levin as an incompetent manager and a cold-blooded opportunist. Levin provided plenty of fuel for his critics with such high-profile failures as Full Service Network, an attempt to develop an interactive television station, which lost $100 million dollars before the plug was pulled. According to an article by Alan Deutschman in *Gentlemen's Quarterly*, "Levin entered into a remarkably stupid deal in 1993 that tied his hands. He sold 25 percent of the company's crown jewels [most valuable assets] to U.S. West for $2.5 billion, ostensibly as part of an effort to pay off Time Warner's debts."

The criticism increased after Levin's inept handling of a controversial song produced by Time Warner. The lyrics of "Cop Killer" by musical artist Ice-T talked about killing police officers. Ignoring his advisers' pleas to apologize and withdraw the record from the market, Levin defended it on grounds of creative freedom and the right to free speech. Ice-T finally withdrew the record on his own, leaving Levin looking out of touch with the world.

Ironically, Levin was far more in touch with his target audience than the average top executive. He and his second wife, Barbara, were avid readers and spent entire weekends watching movies. Sleeping an average of fewer than five hours per night, they made a point of seeing virtually all Warner Brothers movies and television shows and reading as much of Time's printed material as possible.

RISKING HIS NECK

In October 1996, when Levin announced another of his trademark gambles, a merger with Ted Turner's cable television empire, critics pounced again. Many predicted he would be eaten alive by the dynamic personality of Turner. *Fortune* magazine noted that Levin was "risking his very own neck" in the deal. Others openly speculated on how soon Levin would be forced out of his post, particularly when Time Warner's stock prices continued to lag well behind the market. But Levin cultivated the confidence of his board of directors and tenaciously followed his own risky course. When he and Turner eventually clashed, it was Turner who was pushed aside in May 2000, leading Turner to call the merger the biggest mistake of his life.

By the end of the 1990s, Time Warner's stock performance improved enough that Levin was again hailed as an astute company leader. He now not only had control of Time Warner's huge assets, but also had become a dominant player in the cable television industry with Turner's Cable News Network (CNN), E!, and superstation WTBS.

The prudent course for a person in charge of such a huge communications empire would have been to repress his gambling instinct. Levin had risked a tiny company when he took HBO to satellite, but now he stood to lose a colossal corporation worth billions of dollars. The company was on solid footing; there seemed to be no need for extraordinary measures.

But Levin could not resist the lure of the big risk. In explaining his goals to the press, he said, "I finally want to make as clear a break as possible into the future." With that in mind, Levin stunned the business world in 2000 by announcing a new merger, this time with Internet giant America Online (AOL). Hoping to make use of AOL's 30 million subscribers to expand his customer base, Levin risked the world's largest media company on a merger with a company that had been in business only 15 years. Even more surprising, he agreed to the new name of AOL Time Warner, putting the younger company's name first.

Levin's final gamble proved a disaster. AOL Time Warner lost a staggering $99 billion in 2002. Most of the loss was blamed on the AOL part of the business; AOL stock had been overvalued at the time of the merger, and the Internet provider began losing customers. This led AOL founder and AOL Time Warner chairman Steve Case to announce his resignation in January 2003, and the company returned to using the name Time Warner. Levin had already retired six months earlier.

Gerald Levin and Steve Case, chairman and CEO of America Online, announced on January 10, 2000, that AOL would purchase Time Warner for about $163 billion in stock. At the time, it was the largest corporate merger in history.

LEGACY

Gerald Levin may be remembered as one of the most audacious gamblers in broadcasting. He won big, turning HBO from a tiny, struggling network with a two-state distribution area into the largest pay-television service in the world. By the end of the twentieth century, HBO and its sister network Cinemax claimed more than 33 million subscribers and revenues approaching $2 billion per year. It was

Levin, too, who was largely responsible for creating the enormous Time Warner empire that controlled a significant share of what Americans watched and read. He also bore responsibility for having put that giant corporation in grave danger and costing investors and employees billions of dollars.

Levin's primary contribution to the world of media and communication, however, was providing the breakthrough that opened up television. Prior to the mid-1970s, television was dominated by the three major networks (NBC, CBS, and ABC), with only a few local independent commercial and public broadcasting stations offering variety. As a result of Levin's decision to experiment with satellite technology for his HBO network, that situation changed dramatically. When he was making his breakthrough, Gerald Levin predicted that it would open up television programming to the point that there would be hundreds of channels devoted to the most specialized interests. With many cable channels now focusing exclusively on such things as golf, knitting, and gardening, Levin has been proven correct.

4

TED TURNER

CREATOR OF NEWS NOW: CNN

In 1976, the woeful Atlanta Braves baseball team continued to lose under its new owner, Ted Turner. Yet the atmosphere had changed in Atlanta's ballpark. Displaying a combination of creativity and disdain for the establishment, Turner brought an air of excitement even to a bad team.

Before one home game, the team's owner circled the bases riding atop a galloping ostrich. When the Braves suffered their 16th consecutive loss, Turner decided he could do no worse and managed the team himself for the 17th loss. Such antics exasperated the baseball establishment, including league commissioner Bowie Kuhn. At one point, Kuhn demanded of Turner, "Why can't you be like everyone else?"

Robert Edward Turner III (b. 1938) began his broadcasting business with one television channel that relegated the news to a 3 A.M. comedy show. But he changed his mind about covering news, founding CNN in 1980. His all-news network in turn changed the way in which the news was covered.

That question was asked of Turner many times over the years. One close friend described him as "a mixture of a genius and a jackass." Time Warner executive Gerald Levin called Turner "by far the most interesting person I've ever met." The media dubbed him "Captain Outrageous" and "The Mouth of the South." But one thing he had never been was "like everyone else." Ted Turner's relentless drive, explosive personality, and spontaneous creativity made him by far the best-known media network owner of his time. Relishing his role as the folk hero of the average American doing battle against the faceless corporate giants, Turner changed the landscape of television broadcasting.

DOMINATING FATHER

Robert Edward Turner III was born on November 19, 1938, in Cincinnati, Ohio. His life was dominated by his gruff, demanding father, Robert Edward "Ed" Turner Jr. A native of Mississippi who watched his own father lose his cotton farm during the Great Depression, Ed Turner had worked hard and earned his fortune in the billboard business in Ohio. In 1948, he and Ted's mother, Florence Rooney Turner, moved to Savannah, Georgia, where opportunities for the business appeared promising. Concerned about keeping his son in line during the many weeks when his job forced him to be on the road, Ed enrolled Ted in the Georgia Military Academy when the boy was in fifth grade. Arriving at school six weeks into the term and ridiculed for being a Northerner, Ted acted out, getting in frequent fights.

More of the same took place in 1950 when Ed Turner forced Ted to begin attending another private institution, the McCallie School, in Chattanooga, Tennessee. Florence Turner remarked, "Ted hated McCallie. He was a devil there." Rebellious and a loner, he smuggled squirrels and alligators into his room and during his first year was given more than 1,000 demerits, a school record. Ed beat his son frequently in hopes of straightening him out.

Although his father planned for him to take over the family business, Ted harbored dreams of becoming a missionary. But when he was 15, his younger sister, Mary Jane, developed an agonizing case of lupus, a disease in which the immune system attacks the body's own tissue. Although Ted prayed constantly for her healing, Mary Jane suffered for five years before she died. The experience caused Ted to lose his religious faith.

In spite of his many problems at home and at school, Ted grew to appreciate McCallie. He became a capable student who read constantly, as well as an excellent public speaker. Ted's team won the Tennessee state title in a high school debate contest. Whenever he focused on an objective, he pursued it with fierce determination. He took up sailing and worked his way up from bumbling beginner ("Turnover Ted") to the top of his competitive class. But no matter what he did, he could not escape the domineering grip of his father. Although he had dreams of attending the U.S. Naval Academy, he listened to his father and attended Brown University in Rhode Island, instead.

FAMILY TRAGEDIES

Ted Turner's career at Brown was a mixture of great successes and embarrassing failures. As a freshman, he was undefeated in sailboat competition; the following year he was suspended for his involvement in a drunken brawl. After spending six months in the Coast Guard Reserve, he returned to Brown. But when his father learned that Ted planned to major in classical literature, he penned a scathing letter to his son in which he said, "I am appalled, even horrified that you have adopted classics as a major." He called the works of Plato and Aristotle "useless deliberation." Ted responded by publishing the letter in the Brown newspaper. He did later switch his major to economics, but then he was expelled from school for hosting a female student in his dorm room. (Brown was a men's college at the time.)

Meanwhile, Ted's personal life grew difficult. His parents divorced in 1957; Mary Jane died in 1958. After a brief time back in the Coast Guard, Ted went to work for his father. Although he was working as general manager of the Turner Advertising Company's branch in Macon, Georgia, he seemed lost, spending his spare time drinking, gambling, or shooting rifles. He was married, fathered two children, then divorced, within three years.

The worst was yet to come. Ed Turner, who had been plagued by fits of depression in recent years, took a risk by spending $4 million to acquire properties that would make Turner Advertising the top outdoor advertising company in the United States.

After signing the deal, however, he worried that he had spent more than he could afford, then panicked and sold off the business to a friend. He soon regretted doing so. On March 5, 1963, after eating breakfast, he went into his bathroom and shot himself.

ON HIS OWN

Although reeling from the loss of the major influence in his life, Ted Turner stopped the sale of the company and sold his father's plantation to pay some

Ted Turner (second from left) worked for his father's sign company, Turner Advertising.

of the debt. A tough, energetic businessman, he turned Turner Advertising into a multimillion dollar corporation. In 1964, he married Jane Smith, who he met at a political rally. In contrast to his meddling father, Turner paid little attention to their three children, or the two from his first marriage, who also lived with him. He spent his time at work or sailing.

Like many of his business moves, Turner's decision in 1968 to expand his business into radio by buying WAPO in Chattanooga was more of a hunch than a deliberate business plan. But he quickly added stations in Jacksonville, Florida, and Charleston, South Carolina. In 1970, he learned that television station WJRJ in Atlanta was losing money. Against the advice of his financial advisers, he purchased channel 17 and changed the station's call letters to WTCG (Turner Communications Group).

Most observers believed Turner had made a foolish purchase on a station losing $600,000 a year. The station had few viewers, and it operated on UHF (ultrahigh frequency), a wavelength that many televisions were not designed to receive. The station's equipment was outdated and inadequate, operating on a transmission line so badly maintained that it blew up. The station remained off the air for seven days. But as Turner often said, "I just love it when people say I can't do something." Creating a TV lineup largely out of old reruns, he engineered such a dramatic turnaround that his station began showing a profit within a year and a half.

UHF (ultrahigh frequency): a band of radio frequencies from 300 to 3,000 megahertz

VHF (very high frequency): a band of radio frequencies falling between 30 and 300 megahertz

BASEBALL AS A TV PRODUCT

Turner learned in 1973 that the Atlanta Braves were dissatisfied with a meager 20-game contract on a rival Atlanta TV station. Although he knew nothing about baseball, Turner recognized that a baseball team offered popular and profitable programming with very little production expense effort. He dipped deep into his pockets to offer the Braves a 60-game contract, which was accepted.

The Braves soon proved to be a key element of a bold plan that Turner began developing after watching a tiny pay-television service, Home Box Office (HBO), become a national sensation overnight through the use of satellite communications. Turner decided he wanted to use this technology to transform his Atlanta station into a national network. Sending his station's signal via satellite and cable instead of bouncing it off transmission towers allowed people throughout the country to view his programs. This would increase his audience and therefore his advertising revenue tremendously. The cable system would also allow him to charge monthly fees to subscribers.

The problems, however, were daunting. He borrowed heavily to finance the expensive satellite-use fees. He had to obtain approval from the Federal Communications Commission. The broadcasting networks were against his scheme, as were Hollywood studios, which claimed that Turner would be paying the local station price to air their movies, then showing them nationally. But the FCC approved Turner Broadcasting Systems's application and channel 17 turned into the "Superstation," WTBS.

Many parts of the country, particularly in rural areas, had no access to sports programming. Turner bet that these people would be attracted to Braves baseball, particularly if the games were on regularly enough for viewers to become familiar with the players. Unfortunately, the Braves were one of the worst teams in baseball, a fact that reduced their national appeal. Turner, however, turned that situation into a plus. Because they were so awful, Turner was able to buy the team in 1976 at a bargain price. Owning the team allowed him to put 162 games on the air without having to pay for them. Turner acquired even more sports programming a short time later by purchasing the Atlanta Hawks professional basketball team.

The new sports teams owner gained national attention for his eccentric, exuberant behavior, such as greeting players at the plate after they hit a home run. Turner also earned a one-year suspension from baseball for trying to persuade players under contract with other teams to sign with him. He earned even more fame as the captain of the yacht *Courageous*, which he and his crew sailed to victory for the United States in the prestigious America's Cup race in 1977. Some of the publicity was negative, however, and his often tactless behavior saddled him with the nickname "Captain Outrageous."

"There's never been an owner like him. He enjoys it more than anyone in the ball park."
—Phil Niekro, pitcher for the Atlanta Braves

"I'm the little guy's hero. They love me. I run the team the way they think they would if they owned it. I come to all the games. Sit in the stands. Drink a few beers. Even take my shirt off. I'm Mr. Everyman."
—Ted Turner

CNN

In the meantime, Turner's bold venture into cable television looked like a winner. By 1978, WTBS could be viewed in more than two million homes in 45 states. This wide coverage attracted advertising money, especially since Turner charged 30 percent less than the major networks.

Although Turner was famous for his unpredictable nature, his next major project took everyone in the business by surprise. Turner had no interest in the news, and as a result, his TV stations had provided only the minimum news coverage required by law to keep his license. But some new experiences and friends—including fellow Georgian Jimmy Carter, who had become president of the United States in 1977—had helped Turner to develop a desire to be a good world citizen. Now he proposed what seemed like a crazy scheme to create a TV channel of nothing but news, 24 hours a day. Critics scoffed at the idea, which only made him more interested in trying it. "I'll do it because a lot of people in high places laughed at me," he announced.

On June 1, 1980, Turner's Cable News Network (CNN) began broadcasting. At first his critics seemed to be right. Trying to build a national news team large enough to fill 24 hours a day of airtime was a difficult, expensive process. CNN's initial telecasts were often of poor quality, and they attracted few viewers. But with his combination of business management and personnel skills, Turner guided the venture into both respectability and profitability. As

Turner aboard the Courageous. *He took risks on the water just as he did in the boardroom.*

CNN sports reporter Nick Charles said, "He was much more than a cheerleader. He was the kind of guy you'd want to run through a wall for."

Styling himself as just an ordinary citizen doing battle against the three powerful television networks, Turner fought aggressively. When CBS, NBC, and ABC refused to include him in the media pool coverage of the White House, he sued the networks and then President Ronald Reagan's administration—and won. Turner convinced Congress to cooperate with his venture by installing a satellite dish for the House of Representatives and by reminding its members that he could give them far more opportunity than the other networks to express their views on the air.

CNN covered mostly national news until a meeting in 1981 with Cuba's leader Fidel Castro persuaded Ted Turner to transform the station into a global news network. At a time when the major networks were cutting back on their overseas news departments, CNN expanded both its reporting staff and its viewership. By 1982, CNN was on the air in Asia, and three years later it moved into Europe. The supposedly foolish venture had become so large and profitable that in 1985 Turner was in a position to make an offer to buy one of his giant rivals, CBS.

MEDIA GIANT

The deal with CBS fell through, so Turner used the millions he earned from his superstation to collect new programming. In 1985, he spent $1.5 billion to acquire Metro Goldwyn Mayer (MGM), the movie

company. Upon discovering the studio was saddled with massive debts that he could not assume, he sold most of it back within three months. He retained ownership of MGM's library of 3,500 films, however, bringing his motion-picture collection to more than 5,000. He used that collection as a basis for starting two new networks, Turner Network Television (TNT) in 1988 and Turner Classic Movies (TCM) in

Ted Turner appointed Tom Johnson (standing with phone) president of CNN in 1990. During the Persian Gulf War, Turner told Johnson to spend whatever he needed to cover the 1991 conflict.

1994. Typical of Turner, his movie project was not without controversy; he outraged some motion-picture historians by his use of computer technology to add color to films shot originally in black and white. In 1991, Turner purchased the Hanna-Barbera cartoon library, giving him control of one-third of all commercial cartoon shows that had been created in the country. He used this resource to start the Cartoon Network a few years later. It seemed that everything Turner touched turned to gold. Even the bumbling Atlanta Braves dramatically reversed their fortune in the 1980s and became one of baseball's most solid and successful franchises.

Ted Turner made decisions quickly and forcefully, and he stuck to them tenaciously. Although he was once a smoker himself, he made the decision never to hire a smoker. "I figured any young person who's dumb enough to smoke is too dumb to work at CNN or TBS," he explained. After his second marriage ended in 1988, he heard that movie actor Jane Fonda was also recently divorced. On a trip to California in 1989, he asked to meet her. The romance between the flamboyant figures made national news, and the two were married in 1991.

MAN OF PEACE

The relationship with Fonda appeared to help Turner relax for the first time in his life. But in the mid-1990s, Turner's anxiety and restlessness returned. Despite the fact that he now owned TBS, CNN, TNT, Turner Classic Movies, the Cartoon Network, the Braves, the Hawks, and the Atlanta

surrounding the networks he had built. In January 2000, Time Warner was acquired by America Online without any input from Turner. To cap off a disastrous year, Turner and Fonda were divorced and, as the largest shareholder in AOL Time Warner, Turner took a severe hit to his assets when the company's stock floundered. After losing several billion dollars on his stock, Turner dropped out of active management in his old businesses and looked for new projects in which to invest his energies.

LEGACY

Ted Turner was the man who took advantage of the opening Gerald Levin created in using satellite and cable technology to challenge the iron control of the big three networks. He created a half-dozen of the most popular television networks on the air today. Furthermore, he was a major public figure and international philanthropist whose generous contributions enriched the lives of many.

Turner's greatest influence in broadcasting, however, was in creating the 24-hour news channel, CNN. Perhaps the network's defining moment came on January 16, 1991, the start of the Persian Gulf War. Anticipating the war, Turner had spent a fortune building his own communications system in Baghdad, Iraq. His crew there was equipped with two satellite telephones, a portable satellite transmitter, and a special phone line. When war was imminent, he rejected pleas (including one from President George Bush) to order his staff out of Baghdad for fear they would be killed either by

With former senator Sam Nunn, in 2001 Turner created the Nuclear Threat Initiative, which aimed to reduce nuclear, chemical, and biological weapons. He remained active in the Turner Foundation, begun in 1991, which awarded as much as $50 million annually to environmental work.

bombs or by Iraq's dictator, Saddam Hussein. Turner left it up to each staff member whether to stay or leave; eight stayed. As a result, CNN was the sole provider of dramatic, live coverage of the conflict to the entire international community—as many as 60 million people at a time. Other news organizations and even world leaders watched CNN to learn what was happening not only in Baghdad, but also throughout the Middle East.

"When all the smoke from Desert Storm had cleared, it became obvious that the CNN the world had been watching was not just an extension of American domestic television news, but a genuinely global network with a truly international mission whose anchors just happened to live and work in Atlanta, Georgia, U.S.A.," wrote journalist Porter Bibb. "The political and journalistic consequences of what Ted Turner had created were becoming apparent."

In the minds of many, the political consequence of CNN's presence throughout the world has been to make governments more accountable for their actions. CNN reporter Christiane Amanpour argues that CNN has "changed people's relations with their governments. It's meant that governments can no longer crack down with impunity on protests."

The journalistic consequences have been that news is now reported as it happens, not after. Other networks have since copied CNN's format, including the Fox News cable channel and MSNBC, a cable station and Internet news source jointly owned by Microsoft and NBC.

Public Use of the Airwaves

The cable channels created by Ted Turner and Gerald Levin challenged the dominance of the big three commercial television networks, ABC, CBS, and NBC. But there had been an alternate choice for consumers even before cable. It was called public television and, like commercial television, it began with radio.

In 1917, the University of Wisconsin was the first academic institution to attempt educational voice broadcasts with its experimental station 9XM. In 1930, a national group of educational radio advocates urged the FCC to require localities to reserve channels exclusively for educational use. On January 26, 1936, the FCC did establish a class of noncommercial educational radio stations.

Television followed in 1952, when the FCC issued a regulation reserving part of the spectrum for noncommercial television, most of which was in the ultrahigh frequency (UHF) range. The next year, the University of Houston took up the challenge and established the first educational television station, KUHT. In 1962, the federal government began providing support for noncommercial television. Five years later, Congress passed the Public Broadcasting Act, creating the Corporation for Public Broadcasting (CPB) and the Public Broadcasting Service (PBS). Owned and operated by the nation's 350 public television stations, PBS provides programming to its members. Its most popular children's show, *Sesame Street*, debuted on November 10, 1969. About 140 million people watch public television during a given month. In 2005, Congress continued to fund CPB, which in turn supplied PBS with about 15 percent of the funds it needed to operate. State governments, and individual and corporate donations provided the rest of the budget.

National Public Radio (NPR) organized in 1970, also under the terms of the Public Broadcasting Act. The organization began with 30 employees and 90 charter stations. Thirty-five years later, NPR had grown into a major media company, employing 700 people to produce news and entertainment programs for the more than 750 independently operated, noncommercial public radio stations in the United States. A nonprofit organization, NPR charges fees to its member stations to air these programs. In the early twenty-first century, NPR estimated that about 22 million people listened to its shows each week.

5

RUPERT MURDOCH

FOX TV CHALLENGES
THE NETWORKS

Rupert Murdoch's relentless drive for domination in the business of mass communication made him a controversial figure. In the words of one competitor, Sumner Redstone, chairman of Viacom, "He basically wants to conquer the world. And he seems to be doing it."

Murdoch founded the News Corporation, a media company that in 2004 owned the Fox television network and cable and satellite television operations spanning five continents plus the 20th Century Fox film and video companies. News Corporation also published 175 different newspapers in Australia, Britain, New Zealand, and the United States, as well as magazines such as *TV Guide* and books through its company HarperCollins.

Keith Rupert Murdoch (b. 1931) began his media corporation with newspapers, but was soon attracted to the bright lights of television broadcasting and movie making.

During the 1990s, Murdoch influenced a series of acquisitions and mergers among many of the other large media companies that were trying to compete with him—and also trying not to be bought up themselves.

PRIVILEGED LONER

Keith Rupert Murdoch was born on March 11, 1931, in Melbourne, Australia. Rupert, as he was known, was the grandson of a well-known Presbyterian minister who had emigrated from Scotland, and the only son among the four children of Sir Keith Murdoch and Dame Elisabeth Murdoch. Keith, who became a celebrity in Australia because of his work as a correspondent during World War I, was promoted to management in the newspaper business. Elisabeth had won awards for her work in social causes.

Rupert lived a privileged life, bouncing between the Murdochs' comfortable home in suburban Melbourne and their farm about 30 miles outside the city. He spent most of his school years at the prestigious Geelong Grammar School. Later, Murdoch described himself as "a bit dull and humorless, not the sort of person who makes social friends easily." The loner characteristic was one he would retain all his life.

After graduation from Geelong in 1949, Murdoch traveled to England to attend Worcester College at Oxford University. More interested in politics than in his studies, he joined the Oxford Labour Club (the Labour Party was the liberal political party in Great Britain) and "thoroughly reveled in his antiestablishment reputation," according to biographer Richard Hack. Murdoch was reported to have kept a bust of Soviet leader Vladimir Lenin in his room and earned the nickname "Red Rupert."

Avoiding his Father's Mistakes

The comfortable foundation of Murdoch's life shattered, however, in October 1952, when his father died unexpectedly. Murdoch stayed at Oxford to finish his master of arts degree and then accepted an offer from his father's friend, publisher Lord William Beaverbrook, to take a job as an assistant editor for the London *Daily Express*. Ever since he was small, Murdoch loved being at the center of the action in breaking news. While working at the *Daily Express*, he decided that someday he wanted to own and manage that paper.

Believing that he was financially secure, Rupert was stunned to learn that his father had actually left the family with little money. Despite having been head of Australia's number one news organization, the *Melbourne Herald*, the elder Murdoch had not owned much stock in the company and left startlingly little after the estate taxes were paid. Rupert's inheritance was a small, struggling newspaper, the *Adelaide News*. Taking on many of the editorial jobs himself, he applied some of the tricks he had seen used in London, such as huge sensational headlines and aggressive advertising. Before long, his paper was by far the most popular in Adelaide, Australia's third-largest city.

By 1956, Murdoch was ready to unveil the strategy that would serve him time and again as he expanded his influence in media. In acquiring new companies, he would not take on any business partners or investors who might gain control over his business. Instead, Murdoch borrowed whatever money he needed against his assets to take over a media outlet—first newspapers and eventually television stations. He would then apply his marketing techniques to the new business and make it profitable.

EXPANSION

Murdoch's first expansion took him to Perth, where he bought a Sunday newspaper in 1956. Shortly thereafter, he branched out into television with the purchase of channel 9 in Adelaide. In 1960, the 29-year-old Murdoch was ready to tackle his most ambitious project, buying the Sydney *Daily Mirror* and *Sunday Mirror* for $4 million. Sydney, Australia's largest city, was considered one of the most competitive newspaper markets in the world. There Murdoch was opposed by the powerful Packer family, owners of the *Daily Telegraph* and *Sunday Telegraph*, who vowed to drive him out of business. But again, his aggressive sales tactics and sensational, sometimes racy, reporting strengthened the floundering *Mirror* until it was able to hold its own.

In 1964, Rupert Murdoch set his sights higher by founding *The Australian*, his country's first national newspaper. In this case, Murdoch abandoned his usual marketing and editorial practices and gave the paper a more serious tone. The effort consumed most of his time and energy and took 20 years to earn a profit. But his other enterprises continued to grow and expand until by 1968 he controlled newspapers, magazines, and television stations worth more than $50 million.

At this point, Murdoch was ready to test himself against the far stiffer competition and higher stakes of the London press. He began by purchasing the *News of the World*, a Sunday paper that had six million subscribers at the time, making it the largest newspaper in the world. Looking for something else to print on his presses, which were idle six days a week, he then acquired the *Sun*, a bland daily newspaper whose price was low because it was reportedly losing $5 million a year. Murdoch converted the paper to a tabloid style, reducing hard news, focusing on high-interest stories, and inserting gigantic headlines.

tabloid: a newspaper that is smaller in size than a regular paper for ease of reading; usually a publication that also condenses the news and often prints photos and sensational stories

Even British journalists, whose work tended to be more racy compared to the U.S. press, were offended by Murdoch's journalistic style. Murdoch was not shy about using sex to sell newspapers, regularly printing photographs of topless women on page three of the *Sun*. He attracted readers to *News of the World* by obtaining and printing the memoirs of Christine Keeler, a key figure in a sex scandal involving a British government minister and a Soviet naval officer suspected of being a spy. Critics also railed against his casual treatment of the subject of war, such as when he headlined a photograph of the sinking of an Argentine cruiser during the Falkland Islands War "GOTCHA!" But as always, Murdoch's

Murdoch's papers continue to use his design style of banner headlines and large, eye-catching photographs, as seen in these sample front pages from The Daily Telegraph *(Sydney, Australia) and the New York* Post, *all published in December 2003.*

methods increased sales. Within a year, he increased the *Sun*'s circulation from 800,000 to 2 million.

TARGET U.S.A.

Seeking expansion opportunities, Murdoch turned his sights toward the United States. In 1973, he purchased the San Antonio *Express* and *News*, then started *The Star*, a tabloid designed to compete against the *National Enquirer*. None of this satisfied Murdoch's desire to become a major player in journalism.

To accomplish that, he needed a big American paper. In 1976, he grabbed his chance when the New York *Post*, founded by Alexander Hamilton in 1801 and the oldest continuous daily paper in the United States, became available. Murdoch's purchase, for a reported price of $30 million, created a huge outcry of protest. New Yorkers were fearful that Murdoch would sully the paper's outstanding reputation and that his political views, which had changed dramatically since his college days, would influence the paper's content. Although he restrained his usual practices somewhat at the *Post*, the paper soon took on Murdoch's style of flashy headlines and his conservative political slant. In 1982, he added to his American acquisitions, purchasing the *Boston Herald*. The following year he swept into Chicago and bought that city's *Sun Times*.

By this time, Murdoch had shifted his sights from the print media to the electronic media. The process had begun slowly with his television stations in Australia, followed by his investment in London Weekend Television, the company that produced the widely respected TV series *Upstairs, Downstairs*. Such experiences had whetted his appetite for further media expansion. Murdoch's friend John Kluge, chairman of Metromedia—a company that owned independent television and radio stations in Boston, New York, Chicago, Washington, D.C., Los Angeles, Houston, and Dallas—advised him to get into television. Murdoch realized that television, particularly American television, had more potential for profits than newspapers.

To save money and help fund the purchase of 20th Century Fox, in 1985 Murdoch relocated his entire London enterprise to a new printing plant with up-to-date computer-run equipment that would put many printers out of work. When the nearly 5,000 union employees went on strike over this issue, he fired them. The British government backed Murdoch in his dispute with the union. He saved millions of dollars using the new technology and employing fewer workers. The striking printers lost their entitlement to severance pay as well as their positions because they walked off the job.

Murdoch then began developing a plan of attack that caught virtually all industry observers by surprise. He started by negotiating for a U.S. movie studio. When he failed to acquire Warner Brothers, he approached 20th Century Fox, which was floundering after a disastrous run of box office failures. In March 1985, Murdoch struck a deal with Texas oil billionaire Marvin Davis to buy 50 percent of 20th Century Fox from him for $250 million. Shortly after this deal, he and Davis combined forces to purchase Metromedia, in what was the largest sale of independent television stations in history. At the last minute, Davis stunned Murdoch by backing out of the deal. Davis and Murdoch were totally incompatible as partners and it was obvious one of them would have to sell his shares of 20th Century Fox. At one point Davis proposed they flip a coin to see who would buy out the other, but he backed down when Murdoch agreed. Rather than give up on the Metromedia deal, Murdoch took what was for him an enormous gamble, shelling out a total of $2 billion to buy out both Davis's interest in 20th Century Fox and ownership of Metromedia.

Murdoch still had to overcome two more barriers, however, before he could take control. First, there was a U.S. law barring citizens of other countries from owning more than 20 percent of any television station in the country. Having lived in the United States for a number of years, Murdoch solved that problem by becoming a U.S. citizen in September 1985. The stickier problem was a Federal Communications Commission rule that banned single owners from owning both a television station and a newspaper in the same city. Murdoch hoped to obtain an exemption as he had done in similar circumstances in Australia, but he got nowhere. In the end, he was forced to sell his newspapers in New York and Chicago and his television station in Boston.

A New Network

Murdoch then revealed his grand strategy—to combine the 20th Century Fox production units in Hollywood with the six independent Metromedia television stations to form a new national network. Since the early days of television, no one had seriously challenged the big three networks of CBS, NBC, and ABC. So many obstacles stood in the way that it hardly seemed possible for Murdoch's new Fox network to succeed. While the big three covered the entire nation through hundreds of local affiliates, Fox had only six stations. Furthermore, available VHF (very high frequency) stations were scarce, so Fox had to operate on UHF (ultrahigh frequency), which a relatively small number of television sets were equipped to receive.

But Murdoch played on his strengths. Although he had only six stations, they were located in the most densely populated areas of the country, reaching nearly one fourth of the population. He then applied to programming the same aggressive, sensational tactics that had always succeeded in the newspaper business. Fox took more programming chances, including shows that pushed the limits of what was considered acceptable taste. He then used such shows to establish an identity as a bold new network targeting the younger audiences that advertisers wanted to reach.

A few innovative, critically acclaimed programs, such as the cartoon show *The Simpsons*, also helped the network win industry respect and gain audiences. In 1989, Fox aired several shows that attracted more viewers than competing shows on the big networks, including the irreverent situation comedy (sitcom) *Married . . . With Children* and *America's Most Wanted*, a program that aired reenactments of crimes and then invited viewers to call in tips to law enforcement agencies. (They did.) Even as Fox was nibbling away at the market share of its rivals, few considered the new station a serious challenger to the major networks until Murdoch came up with the cash to outbid CBS for the rights to broadcast National Football Conference games in the early 1990s.

While his daring Fox experiment was progressing nicely, Murdoch experienced a scare. After he spent a huge amount of money on a satellite television system in Great Britain, a worldwide recession rocked his empire in the early 1990s. As revenues dropped, Murdoch found himself, for the first time, in financial trouble. On the brink of collapse, he refinanced his debt. As the economy recovered and Fox became more firmly established as a major network, Murdoch's income began to flow, and he was able to reestablish his finances. During the late 1990s, Murdoch's media enterprises enjoyed tremendous success. Most notable was the motion picture

The Simpsons: Fox's Gold Mine

Even with the backing of Rupert Murdoch's billions, the Fox television network faced an uphill battle in its early years because of its limited number of affiliates. One show that helped the new network expand throughout the nation was the brash, highly irreverent cartoon called *The Simpsons*.

The show was the brainchild of cartoonist Matt Groening (b. 1954), whose comic strip Life in Hell debuted in 1980. Television producer James L. Brooks liked the strip and in the late 1980s asked Groening to draw some animated shorts for one of Fox TV's programs, *The Tracey Ullman Show*. Groening created some new characters based very loosely on his own family and the Simpsons came to life.

No one had attempted an animated television show aimed at adults since *The Flintstones* in the 1960s, but Fox executives saw potential for Groening's wacky characters and clever, off-beat humor. His Simpson family Christmas special in 1989 was so well received that Groening was given his own weekly show. An immediate hit, the show attracted celebrities to lend their voices to cartoon versions of themselves on an almost weekly basis. Even his boss, Rupert Murdoch, was featured in one January 1999 episode, "Sunday, Cruddy Sunday."

The Simpsons has become a national phenomenon, generating millions in licensing revenues as well as spectacular ratings and reviews. More than 300 episodes of the show had been produced by 2004.

Cartoon character Homer Simpson, his family, and friends have made appearances as toys, on T-shirts, and in video games such as this Play Station offering.

Titanic, which shattered box office records around the world and won the Academy Award for Best Picture in 1997.

Having established himself as a communications giant on three continents, Murdoch decided to try for four. In 1993, he launched Star TV, a satellite broadcast system, in Asian markets, including China and India. The huge population and growing economy of these countries made this a lucrative venture.

LEGACY

Rupert Murdoch was the first person since the pioneer days of television to successfully challenge the Big Three networks of the United States. Despite laboring under daunting disadvantages, Murdoch built up his Fox Network to be a legitimate competitor of CBS, NBC, and ABC and the most watched television network among young adults in America.

Yet this accomplishment was only a small part of the astonishing global media empire that Murdoch created. One of his former key executives, Andrew Neil, called Murdoch "probably the most inventive, the bravest deal-maker the world has ever known." This talent allowed Murdoch to amass a roster of media companies that included, in addition to the Fox network, 20th Century Fox Film Corporation, book publisher Zondervan, and the London *Times* and *Sun* newspapers. He also controlled 60 percent of the newspaper circulation plus several television stations in Australia. Combined, these businesses generated more than $17 billion in revenue in 2002.

Critics charged that Rupert Murdoch built his empire by marketing sex, vulgarity, sensationalism, and dehumanizing "reality" programming that eroded the values of decent, responsible citizenship. Murdoch dismissed such complaints, insisting that he was only offering readers and viewers a wide array of choices. The war of words underlined the significance of Murdoch's role in the world. Murdoch's vast holdings prompted one of his biographers, Jerome Tuccille, to note "No single individual has ever wielded as much power over the media as Rupert Murdoch does today." Such control put him in a position to influence public opinion to a greater degree than any politician or government official alive.

CATHERINE HUGHES

RADIO ONE: VOICE OF THE BLACK COMMUNITY

When Catherine Liggins Hughes made up her mind to buy a radio station, she refused to take no for an answer. Needing to borrow money for the venture, she pitched her proposal to 32 different banks. Every one turned down her request, yet Hughes had no thought of giving up. "Don't believe it when they say no," she said. "That just means you haven't done a sufficient job of convincing them that they should say yes." After each failure, she went back to her desk and looked for ways to improve her presentation.

On her 33rd attempt, Hughes went to a bank where she spoke to Lydia Colon, who was in her first week on the job. Eager to arrange a loan and sympathetic to the situation of another woman,

Catherine Liggins Hughes (b. 1947) worked hard to turn her love of radio into a successful business. In 2005, her company, Radio One, owned 66 stations, offering programs aimed at black, urban audiences.

113

Transistor radios were pocket-sized, battery-powered radios that used the recently invented transistor instead of large vacuum tubes to amplify sound. Many came with earphones, allowing the owner to listen almost anywhere. The transistor radio became available in the mid-1950s, the time when rock 'n' roll music was becoming popular. The two new arrivals were a perfect match: young people loved the portable radios and radio stations eagerly broadcast the music they wanted to hear.

Colon approved the transaction. Such tenacity fueled Hughes's drive to succeed against daunting odds. Her Radio One empire, based in Lanham, Maryland, became by far the most influential media outlet catering to minority audiences. In the words of Tony Brown, dean of Howard University's School of Communications, "It's really a story of Cathy outworking most people and outthinking most people."

GROWING UP BLACK IN OMAHA

Catherine Elizabeth Woods was born on April 22, 1947, in Omaha, Nebraska. Her father, William, was the first African American to obtain an accounting degree at Creighton University and her mother, Helen Jones-Woods, worked as a nurse. Catherine was nine years old when her parents bought her a transistor radio. She loved listening to musical groups such as the Everly Brothers and the Platters, and she often went to sleep with the radio under her pillow.

Catherine was a fine student. She was the first black person to graduate from Duchesne Academy of the Sacred Heart, a private Catholic school in Omaha with a strict dress code that included white gloves and stockings. At the academy, she experienced a strong current of racism; she was advised to have her parish priest accompany her to a father-daughter banquet rather than bring her father. (The priest made sure, however, that she went with her father.) When Catherine was 16, she became pregnant and married the child's father, Alfred Liggins. She was able to finish school, however, and graduate with her class.

RADIO FROM THE GROUND FLOOR

The birth of her baby, Alfred Charles III, inspired Catherine to go to college and try to make something of herself. Although her marriage soon failed, leaving her to raise Alfred by herself, Catherine Liggins began attending Creighton University part-time in 1966, concentrating on business administration. In 1969, while continuing to take classes at the University of Nebraska-Omaha, she scraped together the money to invest in a small, black-owned local radio station, KOWH. Before long, Liggins was spending far more time at the radio station than at work, and she learned every job involved in running the business.

invest: to put money or other assets into a business with the hope of making a profit in the future

Liggins's work in building up the station caught the attention of Howard University dean Tony Brown. In 1971, despite the fact that she had not finished college, he brought her in to Howard's School of Communications in Washington, D.C., to lecture about her experiences. Brown was so impressed with her energy, creativity, and work ethic that he hired her as sales manager of WHUR-FM, the school's radio station. Liggins succeeded beyond expectations at that task. In 1975, her efforts were rewarded when she was promoted to vice president and general manager.

Once again, Liggins enjoyed spectacular success, primarily due to her innovative programming format. One program, *The Quiet Storm*, was aimed at single young women and featured a deep-voiced, smooth-talking male disc jockey who played love songs. It helped to boost the station's popularity as well as its advertising revenues, which increased from a meager $250,000 to $3 million in 18 months. The show attracted such a huge audience that Liggins asked Howard University to copyright the format. The university declined and, as a result, neither the school nor Liggins benefited from the more than 400 national markets that copied the format.

After increasing WHUR revenue nearly ten times in her brief time there, Liggins moved on to a new challenge in 1978. She was hired to revive a radio frequency in Washington, D.C., that had been unused for 12 years. Liggins renamed the radio station WYCB-AM, built the facility, staffed the station, and got it back on the air. But when the owners ran out of money, she quit and began looking for her own station.

STARTING RADIO ONE

That opportunity came in 1979, when she and her new husband, Dewey Hughes, found Washington, D.C., radio station WOL up for sale. The asking price was just below $1 million. Figuring they would need another one-half million to run the station for a year, Dewey and Catherine had to come up with considerable financing. Catherine's persistence finally secured the large loan they needed. With the $100,000 she and her husband put up and additional money from Syncom Communications Corporation, they were in business.

Making the station profitable was another matter, especially considering Catherine now had to pay more than $10,000 a month in interest in addition to payments on the principal amount of the loan. She faced even more immediate problems. The previous owner had fired all the station's workers, and they had taken revenge by destroying or taking anything of value in the station. The first day her station was on the air, Hughes had to race home and pick up her personal collection of albums so she would have something to broadcast.

Hughes immediately began to make radical changes. Wanting a station solidly connected to the community, she moved the station's offices from its comfortable Georgetown neighborhood into a crime-ridden black neighborhood where a young woman had been murdered a few weeks earlier by a gang. She introduced herself to local gangs. Next, she built a glass booth facing the street so the public could watch the broadcasts as they took place. Hughes then made a drastic change in the station's programming, one that most business experts considered suicidal. "We did a format search," she recalled, "which showed that the one area no one was addressing [for black audiences] was news and information." As a result, she switched the format from music to 24-hour-a-day talk radio. She called her company Radio One and adopted the slogan "Where information is power."

Desperate for advertising dollars, Hughes visited all the store owners in the area, trying to persuade them to buy ads on her station for only $10 per minute. Although people appreciated her personal way of doing business, many were leery of the station's format. Hughes refused to concede that her effort was misdirected; she just worked harder to make it succeed. Although she never had any intention of being an on-air radio personality, in 1981 she began hosting *The Cathy Hughes Show* to fill the morning time slot. As a passionate, inspiring spokesperson for issues that touched the black community, Hughes attracted listeners and earned praise from community leaders.

Catherine Hughes on the air at WOL-AM

TOUGH TIMES

Nonetheless, the station was having a difficult time crawling out of its huge crater of debt. As it continued to lose money, Dewey Hughes began to lose faith. He pleaded with Catherine to sell the station and move with him to California, where he hoped to break into the music industry. When she balked, he finally gave her a deadline and threatened to end their marriage if she did not come with him.

Catherine, however, was too committed to her radio dream to back down. "I don't know if that was a bluff," she commented, but she took decisive action on her own and filed for divorce. She then put herself at even greater financial risk by buying out Dewey's portion of the investment. For the next several years, Catherine Hughes poured her life and soul into her radio station. At one point she gave up her apartment and moved into the station offices. For 18 months she washed up in the public bathroom at the station and cooked her meals on a hot plate. Eventually, she turned one office into an apartment.

One of Hughes's worst problems was trying to accomplish the multiple tasks of being radio manager, hostess, and sales director while still caring for her son. She had to bear constant criticism from family and friends for what she was doing, but she insisted, "I was not letting the city raise my son." Alfred came to the station as soon as school was out, did his homework, and ate meals there. Despite living conditions that would seem impossible to many,

Hughes retained fond memories of those days. "Though now it may sound like a terrible hardship," she said, "I loved being in the station for 24 hours. It was like a mother hen sitting on her egg, waiting for it to hatch."

No matter how hard Hughes worked or how many hours she put into the business, however, she could not get ahead. As the station continued to lose money for six years, her car was repossessed. At one point she had to sell a family heirloom, a rare white gold pocket watch made by her ancestors, to keep the business going. Throughout the worst of times, Hughes took pride in open and honest dealings. She said that if you are honest with people you owe money to, most of them will be patient. She never wrote a check that bounced, and when she did not have enough money to pay a bill, she always called the creditors to let them know how she was doing and sent partial payment. Her honesty paid off.

VOICE OF THE COMMUNITY

Catherine Hughes's investors were both worried by and impressed with her dedication to her work. When she was found living at the station, they provided a professional to give her advice on budgeting and management. They also insisted that she abandon her talk radio format and replace it with music. Hughes agreed to a partial change but retained the morning commute hours for talk.

In 1986, Hughes's accountant showed her a statement that did not have the negative numbers she was used to seeing. She pointed out the "errors" to the accountant, who assured her that the station had actually made a profit.

Radio One became widely recognized for wielding great influence in the community. In 1986, it led a 13-week protest against the Washington *Post* Sunday magazine after it ran what Hughes thought was an unfair cover story on a rap artist accused of murder. The station blasted public utility companies for their practices of shutting off heat to poor people and began soliciting donations for various public service causes. The more Radio One became recognized as the "voice of the community," the more political figures and civic leaders made themselves available for its broadcasts.

Alfred, recently graduated from the Wharton School of Business at the University of Pennsylvania in Philadelphia, was now on hand to help with the day-to-day business operations. On Alfred's advice that Radio One needed an FM signal as well as AM, Catherine bought FM station WMMJ later that year. The $7.5 million asking price required new investors, who advised her that the new station would be profitable only if it played mainstream pop music catering to white audiences. Hughes reluctantly agreed. But after 18 months of watching ratings drop, she scrapped that plan. The station resumed the information, news, and talk format that she had long advocated.

Radio One's broadcasts became even more politically active and controversial in the 1990s. For example, Radio One refused a $500,000 loan from

Alfred Liggins and Catherine Hughes. Liggins literally grew up in the radio business. He started his official career in 1985 as an account manager for WOL-AM, working his way up to become chief executive officer of Radio One in 1997. At that time, Hughes became chairperson of the board and secretary.

the state of Maryland, denouncing it on the air as "blood money," after the Maryland legislature expelled black state senator Larry Young for alleged ethics violations. Hughes then hired Young as a talk show host.

THE FIX-IT EMPIRE

Meanwhile, Hughes had begun expanding her Radio One empire. Her strategy developed out of necessity. As she commented, "We were forced to become a fix-it company because we didn't have the money to buy $50 million stations." She searched for radio stations with meager audience share and revenue in urban areas with large black populations. In 1992, Hughes bought two Baltimore stations as well as WPHI in Philadelphia. Two years later, she added WKYS-FM in Washington, D.C. All the stations were struggling to survive. In each case she carefully studied the market to see what was the most-needed niche and then filled it. She also hired a young, aggressive sales force.

By 1995, Hughes' seven-station business had grown to the point where she finally gave up her 14-year stint as host of *The Cathy Hughes Show*. But that was only the beginning. When the FCC raised the limit on the number of radio stations an owner could operate in a particular market, Radio One went on a buying spree. During 1998 and 1999, the company bought 18 radio stations, aided by a huge influx of cash when Radio One went public and sold shares of stock in the company.

Although Hughes insisted that her son obtain a business degree if he wanted to help her run the company, she credited at least some of her success to her lack of college training. She said she was forced to learn every aspect of the radio business from the ground up: "I honestly think that if I had narrowed myself to one major and minor I would never be where I am today." But she has received honorary degrees from four academic institutions, and in 2001 was honored with the Distinguished Service Award given by the National Association of Broadcasters.

Expanding Ownership

Prior to 1996, the FCC tried to maintain free access to the airwaves by severely limiting the number of radio and television stations that could be owned and/or operated by a single person or company, either nationally or in a specific market. On February 8, 1996, President Bill Clinton signed the Telecommunications Act of 1996, which greatly loosened these restrictions. Limits on the number of radio stations that may be commonly owned were completely lifted. There remained only limits within geographical or market areas. The result of this act was a considerable concentration of power in mass communications. Five years after the bill's passage, the number of radio stations in the United States had increased by more than 7 percent. At the same time, the number of radio station owners dropped by more than 25 percent.

This easing of ownership rules has allowed Radio One to expand rapidly in recent years. But even Radio One's expansion paled compared to the explosive growth of media company Clear Channel Communications. By 2004, Clear Channel had acquired more than 1,200 radio stations.

In June 2003, the FCC further loosened restrictions on multiple media ownership. The new rules lifted the ban against ownership of both newspapers and a television station in the same market, and allowed for ownership of more than one television station in large metropolitan areas. The U.S. Senate Commerce Committee almost immediately held hearings on the new rules and recommended legislation that would return some of the new limits to previous levels. Congress approved overturning the new FCC rules.

LEGACY

Catherine Liggins Hughes stands out as a pioneer African American businesswoman. She was the first black woman to have a company traded publicly on a stock exchange, and her initial public offering of that stock in 1999 raised $172 million, more money than any similar offering by a black-owned company in U.S. history. In 2004, her Radio One enterprise owned and operated 66 radio stations in 22 markets,

RADIO ONE

THE URBAN RADIO SPECIALIST

66 Radio Stations in 22 of the Top 60 African-American Markets

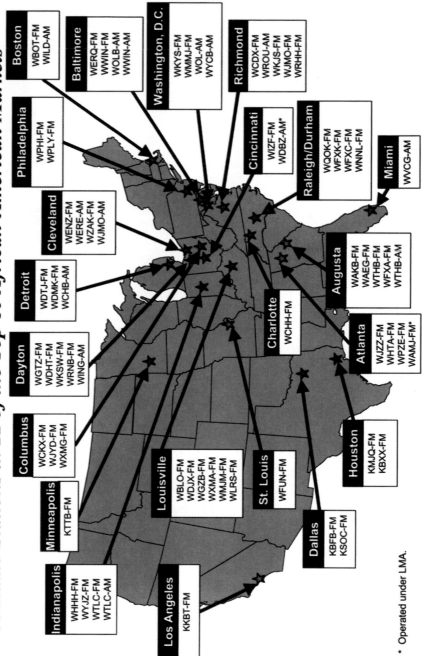

Boston
WBOT-FM
WILD-AM

Baltimore
WERQ-FM
WWIN-FM
WOLB-AM
WWIN-AM

Washington, D.C.
WKYS-FM
WMMJ-FM
WOL-AM
WYCB-AM

Richmond
WCDX-FM
WROU-AM
WKJS-FM
WJMO-FM
WRHH-FM

Philadelphia
WPHI-FM
WPLY-FM

Cincinnati
WIZF-FM
WDBZ-AM*

Raleigh/Durham
WQOK-FM
WFXK-FM
WFXC-FM
WNNL-FM

Miami
WVCG-AM

Cleveland
WENZ-FM
WERE-AM
WZAK-FM
WJMO-AM

Detroit
WDTJ-FM
WDMK-FM
WCHB-AM

Augusta
WAKB-FM
WAEG-FM
WFXA-FM
WTHB-FM
WTHB-AM

Dayton
WGTZ-FM
WDHT-FM
WKSW-FM
WRNB-FM
WING-AM

Charlotte
WCHH-FM

Atlanta
WJZZ-FM
WHTA-FM
WPZE-FM
WAMJ-FM*

Columbus
WCKX-FM
WJYD-FM
WXMG-FM

Minneapolis
KTTB-FM

Louisville
WBLO-FM
WDJX-FM
WGZB-FM
WXMA-FM
WMJM-FM
WLRS-FM

St. Louis
WFUN-FM

Houston
KMJQ-FM
KBXX-FM

Indianapolis
WHHH-FM
WYJZ-FM
WTLC-FM
WTLC-AM

Dallas
KBFB-FM
KSOC-FM

Los Angeles
KKBT-FM

* Operated under LMA.

125

Disc jockey Konan played hip-hop and rhythm and blues music for WERQ-FM listeners in Baltimore, a format used by many Radio One stations. Konan listed his boss, Cathy Hughes, as one of the most interesting persons he ever met, and he shared her strong work ethic. "Every day is pregnant with possibilities for you to be as successful as you want to be," he said. "The choice is yours."

drawing an average of more than 7 million listeners a day. The Radio One empire that she started from scratch was worth in excess of $2 billion and pulled in annual revenues of more than $250 million. Hughes's personal worth was estimated to be greater than $300 million.

Her main goal, however, was not just to accumulate impressive financial figures, but to provide access to information for the mostly inner-city communities in which she broadcast. When asked what drives her in business, Hughes said, "I want to be to the black community what [Washington *Post* owner] Katherine Graham has been to the white community—quality."

Robert Johnson and BET

While Catherine Hughes was filling a void in radio for African Americans in the 1980s, Robert Johnson was doing the same in television. Born in Hickory, Mississippi, on April 8, 1946, Johnson moved to Freeport, Illinois, with his family as a young boy. He obtained a B.A. degree from the University of Illinois in 1968, and a master's degree in international affairs from Princeton University in 1972. He worked in communications and public affairs for the Corporation for Public Broadcasting and for the Urban League, both located in Washington, D.C., and as press secretary for the District of Columbia's U.S. Representative Walter Fauntroy.

Johnson's familiarity with the workings of the federal government helped him obtain the position of vice president of Government Relations for the National Cable and Telecommunications Association, which represented 1,500 cable TV companies across the country. While in this job, he heard a sales pitch for a cable television channel targeting older Americans. It occurred to him that the elderly were not the only underserved segment of society: there was no channel providing programming of special interest to African Americans.

Robert Johnson decided to provide that service. In 1979, he founded Black Entertainment Television (BET), backed by a loan for $15,000. The network made its broadcast debut on January 25, 1980. Forced to operate on a budget that was a tiny fraction of that available to major networks, Johnson aired only a few hours of programming per day—primarily inexpensive, largely unrecognized motion pictures with black actors. In 1982, he added music videos featuring black performers. Over the next several years the network added television shows and a wide variety of music, including hip-hop, jazz, and gospel, until it was providing 24-hour-per-day programming.

Black Entertainment Television lost money each of its first six years. But with the aid of investors, Johnson kept the network afloat until it became profitable in the late 1980s. In 1999, Johnson sold BET to media giant Viacom for $2.3 billion. In 2004, he remained chairman and CEO of the company, and Black Entertainment Television reigned as the leading African American entertainment corporation.

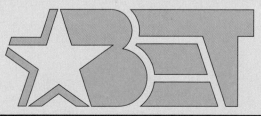

7

JUDY MCGRATH

MTV AND TEENAGE CULTURE

For countless generations, parents have struggled to understand the changes happening to their teenaged children. The drive for independence is a normal part of growing up, but the transition time during which teens break away from the control of their parents and into adulthood has produced tension and exasperation in homes throughout the world. Teens frequently complain that their parents do not understand them, and their parents often agree that teens are beyond understanding. Judy McGrath, however, is one mother who has made a living understanding teenagers. Her uncanny ability to identify the popular styles and interests of America's youth helped build a small music video station into one of the most influential forces in youth culture as well as in television.

Judy McGrath (b. 1952) turned a small cable channel that played music videos into the profitable, influential, and international MTV.

Judy McGrath was born on July 2, 1952, in Scranton, Pennsylvania, the daughter of two social workers, Ann Harding and Charles McGrath. She grew up listening to the big band music of Duke Ellington, her father's favorite performer, but as she grew older, her taste turned to rock 'n' roll. While attending Cedar Crest College, a small women's school in Allentown, Pennsylvania, McGrath became an avid fan of musician Neil Young. She began to dream about someday writing for *Rolling Stone*, the nation's most influential magazine covering rock music.

After Judy McGrath graduated from Cedar Crest with a bachelor's degree in English, her love of music prompted her to take a job working at a radio station in her hometown. She soon switched to magazines in New York City, working first as a copyeditor for *Mademoiselle*, and then as a senior writer and fashion copyeditor for *Glamour*. Next, McGrath began copywriting for National Advertising in Philadelphia. While employed there, she heard about a new cable television company called Warner Amex Satellite Entertainment Company, started by Bob Pittman. Two of her colleagues now working for Warner Amex encouraged her to join them at this company's brand new music channel, called MTV (for Music Television).

McGrath's enthusiasm for music had never faded, and this appeared to be a way to get back into the field, but signing on with the new enterprise seemed a risky career move. "People said, 'Cable television is so tacky and MTV will never last!'" she recalled. "All I knew is they were inventing something and I was attracted to it like it was a shiny object." In 1981, shortly after MTV made its cable TV debut airing a music video—"Video Killed the Radio Star" by The Buggles—she accepted a position as copywriter for on-air programming.

MTV provided an innovative alternative for music lovers, and McGrath came on board at just the right time. She took advantage of the opportunity by showing such a flair for creativity and insight into the target audience that she moved up rapidly within the company. In swift succession during the 1980s, she was promoted to editorial director, then executive vice president and creative director.

FROM BEAVIS AND BUTTHEAD TO POLITICS

While some staff members at the network moved on from the youth-oriented culture in which MTV was immersed, taking other jobs by the age of 30, Judy McGrath seemed to become more comfortable with her job as she grew older. In staying with MTV, she took her cues from her favorite musical artist, Neil Young, who was still performing and vowed to continue doing so as long as people liked what he produced. McGrath's strength as an executive at MTV was that at least part of her never grew up. According to one of her colleagues, McGrath had "a great understanding of what MTV should be. She's truly immature in her heart and she had an extraordinary taste for the bizarre and unconventional."

McGrath's sense of rebelliousness also helped her empathize with her audience. "Every time I try something new and radical, I run into prejudice," she complained. Knowing that young people often feel the same resistance to their attempts at individuality, she declared, "The number one thing I want MTV to always be: A place where young people are appreciated."

McGrath advanced higher than she ever dreamed possible in 1991, when she was named co-president of MTV along with Sara Levinson. As the person ultimately responsible for the network's program content, McGrath recognized that as the novelty of music video television was wearing off, MTV had to come up with fresh programming. In 1992, she gave the go-ahead to two projects that demonstrated the wide range of her vision—from the ridiculous to the serious.

The ridiculous was an animated show featuring two chuckling, witless, adolescent losers named Beavis and Butthead, who criticized various music videos and got into assorted misadventures. MTV hired their creator, Mike Judge, to begin creating regular episodes of the show beginning in late 1992. The crudeness of the humor and Beavis and Butthead's utter lack of redeeming-role-model qualities created an outburst of indignation among parents and various media critics. Teens, however, enjoyed the humor, and the show eventually became a smash hit with all audiences.

In contrast, McGrath that same year initiated a political action project to involve young people in their civic responsibilities. Entitled "Choose or Lose," the campaign attempted to persuade young people that they could influence the condition of society by voting in the upcoming election. The campaign proved to be a great success in turning out the youth vote and, according to McGrath, it was the MTV's irreverent attitude in shows such as *Beavis*

Former vice president and Democratic presidential nominee Al Gore appeared on MTV's Choose or Lose *program during the 2000 election campaign.*

and Butthead that gave it credibility with younger viewers.

"They listen to us because we speak their language, we play their music," she explained. "That puts us in a unique position to put something meaningful in front of them, now and again, about social issues, politics, the world they live in." Because of McGrath's success in ventures such as these, she was given the position of president when Levinson moved on in 1994.

KEEPING UP WITH THE CHANGING CULTURE

One of the challenges of programming for young people was that youth culture changes so quickly, leaving a once-popular format suddenly appearing hopelessly out of date. Judy McGrath showed a remarkable ability to adapt to these wild fluctuations. "A long time ago," she said, "I got over the idea that we will have a crystal clear picture of where MTV is going and adopted a sort of tolerance for uncertainty." Although industry executives considered her an expert in what young people thought and wanted, McGrath knew better than to rely on her own instincts. She made a point of listening to all types of music and watching thousands of videos to stay current with the trends and to understand what was connecting with young people, but she also did her own form of market research. Under her leadership, MTV employed dozens of interns, purposely hiring young people with a wide range of musical tastes, styles, and backgrounds. She gave them free rein to express their opinions without judging them, and she often drew her conclusions about the current youth culture from their ideas. As she stated in 1993, "I try to take my feelings out of it and listen to the researchers, the creative teams, the programmers, and the people who are passionate about music, so it's not just a 41-year-old lady's opinion of everything."

When McGrath and her husband, Mike Corbett, a former banker with the Federal Reserve in New York, adopted a daughter, McGrath discovered that people's expectations of her had changed; they assumed she would lose her enthusiasm or her energy for her job. McGrath disagreed. "If anything," she said, "raising Anna has recharged me." She also found the challenges of parenting provided useful lessons in how to run MTV. Dealing with a small child required her to be nimble, creative, supportive, adaptable, and open-minded—all qualities necessary for coping with the challenges of her fast-paced business.

ANTIVIOLENCE AND THE OSBOURNES

McGrath faced the most serious challenge of her tenure in the mid-1990s, as MTV temporarily lost track of the rapidly changing attitudes and musical tastes. The public began to lose interest in "grunge" music, which had enjoyed a strong run in the early 1990s, and nothing had yet emerged to take its place. Caught in the void, MTV saw its ratings begin to decline. McGrath responded by overhauling the network's programming, introducing shows such as *Total Request Live*, a live music countdown that won

As explained before each episode, The Real World *is "the true story of seven strangers picked to live in a house and have their lives taped." This group of young people lived together in Chicago in 2002.*

back fans. Under McGrath's guidance, MTV also introduced such popular shows as *The Real World*, which was in some ways a forerunner of the spate of reality shows that flooded the market in the early 2000s, and *Unplugged*, which featured acoustic performances by popular musicians.

At the same time, McGrath turned to a mixture of highly praised public service and highly controversial experimental programming. In the public service arena, the network joined forces with the U.S. Departments of Education and Justice and the American Psychological Association to coordinate a campaign against violence. In addition to launching this Emmy Award-winning campaign named *Fight for Your Rights: Take a Stand Against Violence*, MTV hosted more than 600 public meetings in schools and communities across the nation to talk about ways of curbing violence.

The controversy came in the form of a reality television show called *The Osbournes*, in which a camera followed the day-to-day lives of legendary rock singer Ozzy Osbourne and his family. Although sometimes criticized for the Osbournes' profane language, the show proved to be a monster hit in 2001, making it the number one rated program on all of cable that year.

Rock musician Ozzy Osbourne and his wife and two children star in the MTV reality show called The Osbournes. *Ozzy belonged to Black Sabbath, a rock group popular in the 1970s, before launching a solo career.*

LEGACY

Largely under Judy McGrath's guidance, MTV grew into one of the most profitable and influential media companies in the world. After she took over as MTV president, the network more than tripled its annual revenue and became one of the five most profitable U.S.-based media networks. Income for the MTV networks—which grew to include MTV, MTV2, VH1, Comedy Central, Country Music Television (CMT), and the MTV network digital and online music services—more than tripled between 1995 and 2002, surpassing $3 billion annually. (MTV Networks also owns and operates

Nickelodeon/Nick at Nite, Spike TV, and TV Land. Judy McGrath does not, however, work on these channels.)

During the first two decades that McGrath worked at MTV, its viewership skyrocketed from fewer than one million potential households to more than 401 million homes around the globe in 2005. Worldwide, MTV became the most popular cable channel among viewers aged 12 to 24. Each international group of channels—MTV Asia, MTV Australia, MTV Brasil, MTV Europe, MTV Latin America, and MTV Russia—showed a mix of international videos and programs featuring local cultural tastes and musicians.

On a personal level, Judy McGrath shattered the gender barrier in the entertainment communications business. The popularity of MTV and McGrath's influence over what the network put on the air made her perhaps the most important woman in the television business. In 2003, *Fortune* magazine rated her as the 12th most important woman business executive in the world.

McGrath had considerable input into who became a star in the pop culture world. MTV played a major role in launching the careers of such people as Madonna and Britney Spears. Such accomplishments indicate that McGrath did more than merely reflect teen culture; she influenced it in many ways. MTV not only helped shape the music content of the modern generation, but it also inspired trends in television programming and even pioneered new

Teen idol Britney Spears (b. 1982) released her first song "Baby One More Time" in late 1998. Propelled by its video broadcast on MTV, the song hit the top of the Billboard charts, as did the follow-up album by the same name released the next year. Her second album "Oops! I Did It Again" sold one million copies the first week it was available.

concepts in moviemaking, such as the rapid-fire editing that was first seen in music videos.

Because Judy McGrath managed to keep her finger on the pulse of the world's youth for more than two decades, her network was widely considered the most accurate reflection of trends and tastes in teen popular culture. "If you're targeting young people," noted a major advertising executive, "MTV has to be part of your strategy."

Viacom and Redstone: Quiet Giants

At the turn of the century, two of the successful broadcasting businesses featured in this book—CBS and MTV—were owned by Viacom, Inc., the second largest international media conglomerate. Although many of its companies are household names, Viacom itself was pretty invisible to the public.

Viacom was founded in 1971 as a syndication division of CBS. (A syndicate sells television shows directly to independent stations.) The company was spun off two years later when new FCC rules banned television networks from owning syndication companies. In the 1970s and 1980s, Viacom became profitable selling popular old CBS television shows such as *I Love Lucy* and *All in the Family*. The company had enough money to buy Warner Amex Satellite Entertainment, owner of MTV and Nickelodeon, in 1985. Viacom changed the Warner Amex name to MTV Networks.

One year later, National Amusements bought a controlling interest in Viacom. National Amusements owned movie theaters (Showcase and Multiplex Cinemas), and its chief executive officer, Sumner Redstone, became head of Viacom as well. Redstone continued his buying spree in the 1990s, adding Paramount Pictures and the Blockbuster Video stores to Viacom's holdings. In 2000, Viacom bought CBS, its former parent company, in a $50 billion merger. This brought cable channels The National Network (TNN) and Country Music Television (CMT) under Viacom's control. They were made part of MTV Networks. In 2003, TNN was changed to Spike TV, a channel with programming aimed at men. Viacom purchased Black Entertainment Television (BET) in 2001, but that cable channel remained a separately managed company. Other television holdings included Showtime Networks, Inc. (Showtime, The Movie Channel, FLIX, and a partial interest in Sundance) and United Paramount Network (UPN). In 2004, Viacom also held Infinity Broadcasting, which owned and operated 185 radio stations, Simon & Schuster book publishing company, and five theme parks, including Star Trek: The Experience in Las Vegas.

The architect behind Viacom, Sumner Redstone, was not as flamboyant as media moguls Ted Turner or Rupert Murdoch, but he was every bit as intelligent and determined to succeed as his competitors were. Born Sumner Murray Rothstein in Boston in 1923, Redstone graduated from Harvard in the midst of World War II. He joined a U.S. Army intelligence unit that cracked Japan's military codes. When the war was over, he returned to Harvard and earned a law degree. He practiced law for a while, but then in the 1950s he joined the movie theater business his father had founded. A decade later, he was head of the business. In 1979, Redstone survived a hotel fire by hanging out a third-floor window

Viacom chief executive officer Sumner Redstone

with one hand. The other hand was severely burned. Doctors did not expect him to live, much less ever walk again, but Redstone did both.

During his recovery, Redstone began buying stock in Hollywood studios and made millions trading stakes in the big movie companies. (His estimated personal worth in 2004 was $4 billion.) Viacom was initially just another stock investment for Redstone, but he soon realized the company needed new management. He took over Viacom in 1987 and resolved to use the company to make his mark in the movie and broadcasting industries.

Redstone's list of charitable work was as long as his professional resume; many of his activities benefited Jewish philanthropies and arts organizations. He also created and taught an entertainment law course at Boston University School of Law.

WHO OWNS WHAT

Some of the big media companies and their better-known products

CLEAR CHANNEL COMMUNICATIONS

Radio
1,225 radio stations (largest radio broadcaster in the U.S.)

Entertainment
stages 26,000 events annually (concerts, Broadway productions, sports events)

CUMULUS MEDIA, INC.

Radio
240 stations (second largest radio broadcaster in the U.S.)

GENERAL ELECTRIC

Television
Bravo
MSNBC
NBC

HEARST

Television
A&E
History Channel

Newspapers and Magazines
Publishes 12 daily newspapers and more than 100 magazines,

HEARST (CONTINUED)

including:
Cosmopolitan
Good Housekeeping
Houston Chronicle
O the Oprah Magazine
Popular Mechanics
San Francisco Chronicle
Seattle Post-Intelligencer

NEWS CORPORATION

Television
Fox Broadcasting Company
Fox Movie Channel
Fox News Channel
Fox Sports Channel

Motion Pictures
20th Century Fox

Newspapers
Publishes 175 different newspapers in Australia, the United Kingdom, New Zealand, and the United States, plus magazines such as
TV Guide

Books
HarperCollins
Zondervan

TIME WARNER

Television
Cartoon Network
Cinemax
CNN
HBO
Turner Classic Movies

Motion Pictures
Warner Brothers Pictures

Internet/Cable Services
America Online
Earthlink
MapQuest
Moviefone
Netscape
Road Runner
Time Warner Cable

Magazines
Time, Inc., publishes more than 130 magazines including:
Entertainment Weekly
Money
People
Popular Science
Sports Illustrated
Time

Books
Little, Brown, and Company
Warner Books

VIACOM, INC.

Television
BET
CBS
MTV
Showtime
UPN

Radio
Infinity Broadcasting (185 radio stations)

Motion Pictures
Blockbuster video stores
Paramount Pictures

Books
Simon & Schuster

WALT DISNEY COMPANY

Television
ABC
Disney Channel
ESPN

Radio
64 stations

Motion Pictures
Miramax Films
Touchstone Pictures
Walt Disney Pictures

Books
Hyperion Books
Walt Disney Book Publishing

GLOSSARY

amplify: to increase strength

amplitude: the greatest height or strength reached by a wave

AM (amplitude modulation): to encode a radio wave by varying the amplitude (strength) of the wave

anode: an electrode through which current passes from the metallic to the non-metallic conductor; the positively charged electrode. *See also* **cathode, conductor**

antenna: an apparatus for sending and receiving electromagnetic waves

audion: Lee de Forest's radio tube, a variation of the Fleming valve vacuum tube

battery: connected cells that produce an electric current by converting chemical energy into electrical energy

cathode: an electrode through which current passes from the nonmetallic to the metallic conductor; the negatively charged electrode. *See also* **anode, conductor**

cathode-ray tube: a vacuum tube into which a cathode emits electrons that are in turn passed through an anode and then focused on a glowing screen; used in television sets

conductor: a substance that allows the transmission of an electric charge

electricity: power generated by the interactions of positively and negatively charged particles (protons and electrons) in atoms

electrode: an electric conductor through which an electric current passes; cathodes and anodes are types of electrodes

electromagnet: a piece of iron wrapped in insulated wire that becomes magnetic when an electrical current runs through the wire

electromagnetic field: a field around an electric charge in motion that has both electric and magnetic components

electromagnetic wave: a wave of electrical and magnetic energy that travels through space. Light waves, radio waves, and X rays are all electromagnetic waves.

electron: a particle in the atom that has a negative electrical charge

Federal Communications Commission (FCC): the government agency that oversees radio and television broadcasting

Fleming valve: a vacuum tube containing a small metal plate and a filament; when the tube is hooked up to a receiving aerial, an electrical charge flows between the filament and the metal plate inside; used in early radio technology

FM (frequency modulation): to encode a radio wave by varying its frequency

frequency: the number of times a specific phenomenon—such as an electromagnetic wave pulse—repeats itself in one second

gross income: total revenue in a business before any expenses or deductions

iconoscope: an early electronic television transmitter

initial public offering (IPO): a corporation's first offering of its stock for sale to the public

interest: the cost of using credit or another's money, expressed as a rate per period of time, such as 5 percent per year

Internet: an international network that allows computers to exchange information

invest: to put money or other assets into a business with the hope of making a profit in the future

license: to grant another the right to produce and sell an invention for a fee

magnet: an object that attracts iron or steel and is surrounded by a magnetic field

magnetic field: an area of measurable magnetic force surrounding a magnet or electric current

media: the forms of mass communication, such as newspapers, radio, or television, as well as the journalists and broadcasters who work for these organizations

merger: an agreement that combines two or more corporations into one

Morse code: a code of dots and dashes representing letters that Samuel Morse developed to use with the telegraph

network: a chain of radio or television broadcasting stations linked together, or the company that produces the programs for these stations

online: connected to a computer network

patent: the exclusive right, enforced by government, to produce and sell an invention for a period of time

principal amount: the value of an obligation, such as a bond or loan, that must be repaid

radio: a device used to transmit and receive electromagnetic wave signals (radio waves) that range in frequency from 10 kilohertz to 300,000 megahertz

receiver: a device that is designed to receive an electric signal and translate it into recognizable forms such as sound or print

revenue: the amount of money collected by a business

royalty: a share of the income earned on a product that is paid to an inventor in return for the right to manufacture and sell the invention

station: a broadcast organization equipped to transmit radio or television signals; also refers to the frequency assigned to such a broadcaster

stock: shares of ownership of a corporation

stock exchange: an organized marketplace where stocks of companies are bought and sold

subsidiary: a company owned by another company

tabloid: a newspaper that is smaller in size than a regular paper for ease of reading; usually a publication that also condenses the news and often prints photos and sensational stories

telecommunications: the electronic systems used to transmit messages by cable, radio, telegraph, telephone, and television

telegraph: a device that, when connected to other telegraphs by wire, transmits and receives electrical signals in Morse code; a wireless telegraph can send and receive the electronic signals of Morse code through the air

telegraph key: the hand tool used by a telegraph operator to tap out a Morse code message

telephone: a device that converts sound waves into electronic signals, which can be transmitted and reconverted into sound waves to permit conversation

television: a device that receives an electronic signal and converts that signal into an image

transmitter: a device that generates and sends an electronic signal

UHF (ultrahigh frequency): a band of radio frequencies from 300 to 3,000 megahertz. *See also* **VHF (very high frequency)**

VCR (videocassette recorder): an electronic device for recording video images and sound on a videotape. Once the images have been recorded, the VCR can play the tape on a television screen.

VHF (very high frequency): a band of radio frequencies falling between 30 and 300 megahertz. *See also* **UHF (ultrahigh frequency)**

wavelength: the distance between the peak of one wave and the peak of the next corresponding wave

wireless communication: sending and receiving electronic signals through the atmosphere

BIBLIOGRAPHY

"About Radio One." http://www.radio-one.com/about_radio_one.htm, cited June 9, 2003.

Ali, Lorraine, and Devin Gordon. "We Still Want Our MTV." *Newsweek*, July 23, 2001.

Auletta, Ken. *The Highwaymen: Warriors of the Information Superhighway*. New York: Random House, 1997.

———. "The Lost Tycoon." *New Yorker*, April 23, 2001.

Bibb, Porter. *It Ain't as Easy as it Looks: Ted Turner's Amazing Story*. New York: Crown, 1993.

Carsey, Marcy, and Tom Werner. "David Sarnoff." *Time*, December 7, 1998.

"Catherine Hughes." *Current Biography Yearbook 2000*. New York: H. W. Wilson, 2000.

"Catherine Liggins Hughes." *KIP Business Report*. kipbusinessreport/cover_story%2006, June 14, 2002

Chenoweth, Neil. *Rupert Murdoch: The Untold Story of the World's Greatest Media Wizard*. New York: Crown, 2002.

The David Sarnoff Library. "David Sarnoff: Timeline." http://www.davidsarnoff.org/dsindex.htm, cited July 10, 2003.

Deutschman, Alan. "The Ted and Jerry Show." *Gentlemen's Quarterly*, December 1997.

Duncan, Jacci, and Jane Lawrence Sheldon. *Making Waves: The 50 Greatest Women in Radio and Television*. Kansas City: Andrews McMeel, 2001.

Ghosh, Chandrani. "The Comeback Queen." *Forbes*, September 20, 1999.

Goldberg, Robert, and Gerald Jay Goldberg. *Citizen Turner: The Wild Rise of an American Tycoon*. New York: Harcourt Brace, 1995.

Hack, Richard. *Clash of the Titans: How the Unbridled Ambition of Ted Turner and Rupert Murdoch Has Created Global Empires that Control What We Read and Watch*. Beverly Hills, Calif.: New Millennium Press, 2003.

Halberstam, David. *The Powers That Be*. New York: Knopf, 1978.

Henry, William A., III. "Shaking Up the Networks." *Time*, August 9, 1982.

Hoban, Phoebe. "She Wants Her MTV." *Harper's Bazaar*, January 1995.

Klein, Alec. *Stealing Time: Steve Case, Jerry Levin, and the Collapse of AOL Time Warner*. New York: Simon & Schuster, 2003.

Levin, Gerald. "Media and Entertainment." *Vital Speeches of the Day*, February 1, 1998.

Lewis, Tom. *Empire of the Air: The Men Who Made Radio.* New York: HarperCollins, 1991.

MacDonald, J. Fred. *One Nation Under Television.* New York: Pantheon, 1990.

Moritz, Charles, ed. "Rupert Murdoch." *Current Biography Yearbook 1977.* New York: H. W. Wilson, 1977.

Norment, Lynn. "Ms. Radio." *Ebony*, May 2000.

O'Neal, Michael. "The Unlikely Mogul." *Business Week*, December 11, 1995.

Painton, Priscilla. "The Taming of Ted Turner." *Time*, January 6, 1992.

Paper, Lewis J. *Empire: William S. Paley and the Making of CBS.* New York: St. Martin's Press, 1987.

Parshall, Gerald. "Captains of Consciousness." *U.S. News & World Report*, June 1, 1998.

"Reflections on Success." *The Black Collegian Online*, www.black_college.com/issues/30thAnnual.

Saporito, Bill. "Time for Turner." *Time*, October 21, 1996.

Schwartz, Nelson D. "Suddenly Jerry Levin's Stock is Hot." *Fortune*, March 30, 1998.

Shawcross, William. *Murdoch.* New York: Simon & Schuster, 1993.

Skow, John. "Vicarious Is Not the Word." *Time*, August 9, 1982.

Slater, Robert. *This . . . Is CBS: A Chronicle of 60 Years.* Englewood Cliffs, N.J.: Prentice Hall, 1988.

Smith, Sally Bedell. *In All His Glory: The Life of William S. Paley.* New York: Simon & Schuster, 1990.

Stashower, Daniel. *The Boy Genius and the Mogul: The Untold Story of Television.* New York: Random House, 2002.

"This is NBC." http://www.nbc.com/nbc/header/Corporate_Info.shtml, cited June 12, 2003.

Tuccille, Jerome. *Rupert Murdoch.* New York: Donald I. Fine, Inc., 1989.

"TV's Newest Mover and Shaker." *U.S. News & World Report*, May 20, 1985.

Walker, Andrew. "Rupert Murdoch: Bigger than Kane." news.bbc.co.uk/1/low/uk/2162658.stm, cited July 31, 2002.

Whittemore, Hank. *CNN: The Inside Story.* Boston: Little, Brown, 1990.

Source Notes

Quoted passages are noted by page and order of citation.

Introduction

p. 16: Gerald Parshall, "Captains of Consciousness," *U.S. News & World Report*, June 1, 1998, 62.

p. 17 (all): Parshall, "Captains of Consciousness," 62.

Chapter One

p. 22 (margin): Tom Lewis, *Empire of the Air: The Men Who Made Radio* (New York: HarperCollins, 1991), 92.

p. 22: Lewis, *Empire of the Air*, 93.

p. 24 (margin): Lewis, *Empire of the Air*, 105.

p. 25 (caption): Lewis, *Empire of the Air*, 105.

p. 26: Lewis, *Empire of the Air*, 115.

p. 29 (margin): Daniel Stashower, *The Boy Genius and the Mogul: The Untold Story of Television* (New York: Random House, 2002), 79.

p. 31: David Halberstam, *The Powers That Be* (New York: Knopf, 1978), 126.

p. 32 (first): Marcy Carsey and Tom Werner, "David Sarnoff," *Time*, December 7, 1998, 90.

p. 32 (second): Parshall, "Captains of Consciousness," 62.

p. 35: Carsey and Werner, "David Sarnoff," 88.

pp. 40-41: J. Fred MacDonald, *One Nation Under Television* (New York: Pantheon, 1990), 31.

p. 41 (margin): Carsey and Werner, "David Sarnoff," 90.

p. 41: Lewis, *Empire of the Air*, 275.

Chapter Two

p. 43 (caption): Robert Slater, *This . . . Is CBS: A Chronicle of 60 Years* (Englewood Cliffs, N.J.: Prentice Hall, 1988), 156.

p. 43: Sally Bedell Smith, *In All His Glory: The Life of William S. Paley* (New York: Simon & Schuster, 1990), 14.

p. 46: Halberstam, *The Powers That Be*, 21.

p. 47 (margin): Lewis J. Paper, *Empire: William S. Paley and the Making of CBS* (New York: St. Martin's Press, 1987), 23-24.

p. 47: Slater, *This . . . Is CBS*, 10.

p. 48: Slater, *This . . . Is CBS*, 13.

p. 55: Paper, *Empire*, 75.

p. 56: Slater, *This . . . Is CBS*, 46.

p. 61 (first): Smith, *In All His Glory*, 18.

p. 61 (second): Smith, *In All His Glory*, 19.

p. 62: Halberstam, *The Powers That Be*, 23.

Chapter Three

p. 67 (first): Michael O'Neal, "The Unlikely Mogul," *Business Week*, December 11, 1995, 90.

p. 67 (second): O'Neal, "The Unlikely Mogul," 90.

p. 71: Gerald Levin, "Media and Entertainment," *Vital Speeches of the Day*, February 1, 1998, 249.

p. 74: O'Neal, "The Unlikely Mogul," 91.

p. 75: O'Neal, "The Unlikely Mogul," 94.

p. 76 (first): Alan Deutschman, "The Ted and Jerry Show," *Gentlemen's Quarterly*, December 1997, 129.

p. 77 (second): Nelson D. Schwartz, "Suddenly Jerry Levin's Stock is Hot," *Fortune*, March 30, 1998, 104.

p. 78: O'Neal, "The Unlikely Mogul," 87.

Chapter Four

p. 81: John Skow, "Vicarious Is Not the Word," *Time,* August 9, 1982, 57.

p.82 (first): Ken Auletta, "The Lost Tycoon," *New Yorker*, April 23, 2001, 140.

p.82 (second): Auletta, "The Lost Tycoon," 140.

p.83: Porter Bibb, *It Ain't as Easy as it Looks: Ted Turner's Amazing Story* (New York: Crown, 1993), 18.

p.84 (first): Bibb, *It Ain't as Easy*, 29.

p. 84 (second): Bibb, *It Ain't as Easy*, 30.

p. 86: Hank Whittemore, *CNN: The Inside Story* (Boston: Little, Brown, 1990), 14.

p. 88 (margin, first): Bibb, *It Ain't as Easy*, 105.

p. 88 (margin, second): Bibb, *It Ain't as Easy*, 105-106.

p. 89: Whittemore, *CNN: The Inside Story*, 4.

p. 90: Auletta, "The Lost Tycoon," 148.

p. 92: Auletta, "The Lost Tycoon," 149.

p. 93 (first): Auletta, "The Lost Tycoon," 138.

p. 93 (second): Auletta, "The Lost Tycoon," 140.

p. 96 (first): Bibb, *It Ain't as Easy*, 379-380.

p. 96 (second): Auletta, "The Lost Tycoon," 141.

Chapter Five

p. 99: Ken Auletta, *The Highwaymen: Warriors of the Information Superhighway* (New York: Random House, 1997), 260.

p. 100: Charles Moritz, ed., *Current Biography Yearbook* 1977 (New York: H. W. Wilson, 1977), 302.

pp. 100-101: Richard Hack, *Clash of the Titans: How the Unbridled Ambition of Ted Turner and Rupert Murdoch has Created Global Empires that Control What We Read and Watch.* (Beverly Hills, Calif.: New Millennium Press, 2003), 36.

p. 110 (first): Andrew Walker, "Rupert Murdoch: Bigger than Kane," news.bbc.co.uk/1/low/uk/2162658.stm, July 31, 2002, 3.

p. 111 (second): Jerome Tuccille, *Rupert Murdoch* (New York: Donald I. Fine, Inc., 1989), xiv.

Chapter Six

p. 113: "Catherine Liggins Hughes," *KIP Business Report*, kipbusinessreport/cover_story%2006, June 14, 2002.

p. 114: "Catherine Hughes," *Current Biography Yearbook 2000*, (New York: H. W. Wilson, 2000), 304.

p. 117: "Catherine Hughes," *Current Biography*, 304.

p. 119 (first): "Catherine Hughes," *Current Biography*, 304.

p. 119 (second): Lynn Norment, "Ms. Radio," *Ebony*, May 2000, 106.

p. 120: "Catherine Liggins Hughes," *KIP*.

p. 122: "Catherine Hughes," *Current Biography*, 305.

pp. 122-123: Chandrani Ghosh, "The Comeback Queen," *Forbes*, September 20, 1999, 86.

p. 123: "Reflections on Success," *The Black Collegian Online*, www.black_college.com/issues/30thAnnual, 1.

p. 126 (caption): "Q-Jays," http://www.92qjams.com/html/Konan.htm, cited February 1, 2004.

p. 126: "Catherine Hughes," *Current Biography*, 303.

Chapter Seven

p. 131 (both): Phoebe Hoban, "She Wants Her MTV," *Harper's Bazaar*, January 1995, 48.

p. 132 (first): Jacci Duncan and Jane Lawrence Sheldon, *Making Waves: The 50 Greatest Women in Radio and Television* (Kansas City: Andrews McMeel, 2001), 185.

p. 132 (second): Duncan, *Making Waves*, 185.

p. 134 (first): Duncan, *Making Waves*, 185.

p. 134 (second): Duncan, *Making Waves*, 186.

p. 135 (first): Hoban, "She Wants Her MTV," 46.

p. 135 (second): Duncan, *Making Waves*, 185.

p. 136 (caption): MTV, "The Real World," http://www.mtv.com/onair/realworld/.

p. 139: Lorraine Ali and Devin Gordon, "We Still Want Our MTV," *Newsweek*, July 23, 2001, 53.

INDEX

McGrath, Judy: early years of, 130; education of, 130; interest of, in music, 130-131; MTV programs implemented by, 132-134, 135-137; as president of MTV, 134-139; promotions received at MTV, 131, 132, 134; success of, 134, 137-138; and understanding of youth culture, 129, 131, 133-135; work of, for magazines, 130; work of, for MTV, 130-131

Mademoiselle, 130

Madonna, 138

Manchester Guardian, 16

Marconi, Guglielmo, 10-12, 23, 24, 33

Marconi Wireless Telegraph Company, 23-26, 27

Married . . . With Children, 108

Maxwell, James Clerk, 10

Melbourne Herald, 101

Metro Goldwyn Mayer (MGM), 90-91

Metromedia, 105, 106, 107

Microsoft, 96

microwaves, 68-69

Minow, Newton, 17

Montrose, 7-8

Morse, Samuel Finley Breese, 9

Morse Code, 9, 11-12, 23

MSNBC, 96

Munroe, J. Richard, 75

Murdoch, Dame Elisabeth (mother), 100

Murdoch, Sir Keith (father), 100, 101

Murdoch, Keith Rupert, 93, 109, 140; acquisition of newspapers, 102, 103, 104-105; acquisition of electronic media, 105-106; business practices of, 99-100, 102, 103-104, 106; control over the media, 99-100; 111; early years of, 100; education of, 100, 101; establishment of Fox Network, 107-108; establishment of News Corp., 99-100; establishment of Star TV, 110; financial problems of, 101, 108; journalistic style of, 101, 102, 103-104, 105; personality of, 100-101; success of, 108, 109, 110; television programming style of, 107-108, 111; work of, on newspapers, 101, 102

Murrow, Edward R., 54-55

Music Television (MTV), 129, 140; establishment of, 130-131; networks of, 137-138; programming of, 131-137; success of, 137-138

National Amusements, 140

National Association of Broadcasters, 123

National Broadcasting Company (NBC), 21, 22, 35, 38, 40, 44, 46, 47, 48, 50, 52, 53, 58-59, 60, 62, 79, 93, 96, 97, 107, 110; Blue, 31, 41; coverage of the World Series, 39, 58; formation of, 30; MSNBC, 96; programming of, 49, 56, 90; Red, 31; television stations, 38

National Enquirer, 104

The National Network (TNN), 140

National Public Radio (NPR), 97

New York *Post*, 104, 105, 107

New York *Times*, 43

New York World's Fair, 16, 35, 38

The New Yorker, 76

News of the World, 103

Niekro, Phil, 88

Nicolas, Nicolas J., Jr., 74-75

9XM, 97

Nuclear Threat Initiative, 95

Nunn, Sam, 95

Oersted, Hans Christian, 9

Olympics (1980), 93-94

Oops! I Did It Again, 139

Osbourne, Ozzy, 137

The Osbournes, 137

Paley, Goldie Drell (mother), 44

Paley, Isaac (grandfather), 44

Paley, Jake (uncle), 45-46

Paley, Samuel (father), 44, 45-46, 47, 48

ABOUT THE AUTHOR

Nathan Aaseng is an award-winning author of more than 100 fiction and nonfiction books for young readers. He writes on subjects ranging from science and technology to business, government, politics, and law. Aaseng's books for The Oliver Press include seven titles in the **Business Builders** series and nine titles in the **Great Decisions** series. He lives with his wife, Linda, and their four children in Eau Claire, Wisconsin.

PHOTO CREDITS

The Cable Center: pp. 64, 71, 72, 73

CBS Photo Archive: pp. 57, 60

Library of Congress: pp. 9, 10, 14, 19, 25 (bottom), 29, 30, 36, 38, 42, 49, 51, 54, 55, 56, 59

Marconi Corporation, plc.: p. 6

Marylandia Collection, University of Maryland: p. 34

MTV Networks: pp. 128, 133, 136. (Photos of "Judy McGrath," MTV's "Real World: Chicago," and MTV's "Choose or Lose" used with permission by MTV: Music Television. ©2004 MTV Networks. All rights reserved. MTV: Music Television, all related titles, characters, and logos are trademarks owned by MTV Networks, a division of Viacom International, Inc.)

National Aeronautics and Space Administration (NASA): p. 69

Pavek Museum of Broadcasting: pp. 13, 28

Radio One: pp. 112, 118, 122, 125, 126

Revilo: pp. 75, 104, 109, 139

David Sarnoff Library, Princeton, N.J.: front cover, pp. 11, 17, 20, 25 (top), 40

Texas Instruments: p. 114

Turner Foundation, Inc.: pp. 2, 80, 85, 89, 91, 94, back cover

Viacom: p. 141

United Nations: p. 98

Rick Wacha: pp. 12, 37